MICK'S Archaeology

Mick Aston

TEMPUS

First published 2000

PUBLISHED IN THE UNITED KINGDOM BY:

Tempus Publishing Ltd
The Mill, Brimscombe Port
Stroud, Gloucestershire GL5 2QG

PUBLISHED IN THE UNITED STATES OF AMERICA BY:

Tempus Publishing Inc.
2 Cumberland Street
Charleston, SC 29401

Tempus books are available in France, Germany and Belgium
from the following addresses:

Tempus Publishing Group
21 Avenue de la République
37300 Joué-lès-Tours
FRANCE

Tempus Publishing Group
Gustav-Adolf-Straße 3
99084 Erfurt
GERMANY

Tempus Publishing Group
Place de L'Alma 4/5
1200 Brussels
BELGIUM

British Library Cataloguing in Publication Data.
A catalogue record for this book is available from the British Library.

ISBN 0 7524 1480 1

Typesetting and origination by Tempus Publishing.
PRINTED AND BOUND IN GREAT BRITAIN.

Contents

List of illustrations

Foreword

One fateful day in 1985, a brown envelope dropped unbidden onto my doormat. It was a prospectus from the University of Bristol, and it listed the various extra-mural courses available that year. One of those courses was to change my life.

'Expedition to Santorini' it said. 'Discover the island's unique geomorphology, and study the archaeology of its ancient proto-Minoan inhabitants!' 'A week in the sun-kissed Aegean?' I thought. 'Retzina, kebabs and the occasional proto-Minoan.' I sent off my cheque the same night.

And it was on Santorini that I met Mick Aston. I'd always been daunted by archaeology. To me it had meant only dusty museum cases and unreadable books. Mick made the ancient world leap out of the trench and straight into my imagination. It was a world full of people I cared about. They got on with life – moaned about the weather, argued over the garden fence, had a good time and then regretted it the next morning. Mick wasn't much interested in kings and queens – past or present. He wanted to tell today's ordinary people about yesterday's ordinary people. This was his passion and in a way it was mine too. By the end of the week we were friends for life.

When we got back to England I tried to set up a TV series in which Mick would teach me about various aspects of archaeology. Nobody was interested. 'Who'd want to watch a comedian and a boffin being serious about a boring subject?' was the inevitable response. So, like Achilles, I thought 'stuff you!' and retired to my tent.

But as the years passed Mick became something of a celebrity. Five years after our first meeting he was offered his own four-part TV series, *Time Signs*. "I'm very pleased for you" I said, and nearly meant it.

Then another series beckoned – *Time Team*. Mick magnanimously volunteered me as presenter. And the rest, as they say, is archaeology.

Within a year, the Time Team were household faces – Carenza Lewis, the waspish but beautiful Amazon; Phil Harding – a Noddy Holder look-alike with the accent of a Thomas Hardy farm-labourer, but most celebrated of all, the man who holds the entire enterprise together, our leader, Professor Mick Aston – an ancient womble with a terrible taste in knitwear. His passion and

Mick Aston with Tony Robinson

commitment dominate the programme. He never gives orders, he leads by example. His intuitive understanding of a landscape never ceases to amaze us. Without Mick, I doubt if *Time Team* would have got beyond the pilot programme.

That's enough flattery – now the gossip. He hates getting out of bed in the morning, and he's a moody monster 'til he's had his second cup of coffee. He's a dreadful musical snob, a man of Rabelaisian appetites, yet the sort of self-righteous anti-smoker who makes you want to light a Marlboro just to wind him up. He's a born again vegetarian and moans non-stop if he's in a restaurant that doesn't serve the sort of food of which he approves, like squashed beans with nettle sauce. He's also generous, loyal and completely unswayed by the material things in life. And he's three weeks older than me, and pulls rank every chance he can get. There are some people who enhance your life. Mick is one of those people, though I'd never tell him to his face.

Please turn the pages and meet my friend.

Tony Robinson

Introduction

I have been involved in archaeology in one way or another for thirty-five years and I have spent over thirty years teaching archaeology to extra-mural and continuing education classes, in Birmingham, Oxford and Bristol; over the last ten years I have been mainly occupied with making television programmes about archaeology. In all these activities I have been trying to explain what archaeology is about, why I find it so passionately interesting and why I think the past is so important now and what it can mean for us in the future.

All through this period I have been asked many times, especially as I became more involved with the 'media', about how I first became interested in archaeology, what I have done in my career, which periods and subjects most interest me, which sites I have felt most excited about, which books I would recommend and so on. I have answered these questions as honestly as I could but all the time I have felt that I really should write it all down – if only to make available what others tell me is my infectious enthusiasm for the subject, to as wide a readership as possible. This little book is my first attempt to do so. I hope the reader will not only enjoy it but feel enthused by it.

This is not a book about *Time Team*. But after nearly a decade during which an increasing amount of my time has been devoted to the making of *Time Team* programmes, so that now it takes at least nine months of each year, it is impossible, and not realistically advisable to exclude it. *Time Team* is now a television and archaeological phenomenon, complete with its own fan club and groupies. So what I have tried to do here is show where the making of the television programmes fits into *my* archaeology. I hope I have given the right perspective.

I shall be happy to receive letters of encouragement (or otherwise) in case there is ever a chance to do a revised edition.

Mick Aston
Sandford, Somerset
1 August 1999 (St Aethelwold of Abingon's Day)

1 Early years in archaeology

The start of my headlong career through archaeology was both late and conventional. Although my parents, and especially my father, were interested in old 'things', whether it was places, objects, buildings or sites, and we had visited many places in Cornwall on holidays, it was not until I was about sixteen that I showed a real interest. I have always been a late developer in everything, so this must be the equivalent of about twelve or so in anyone else. I cannot claim to have always wanted to be an archaeologist since I was a child. For much of the time I was going to be a teacher: by the end of the sixth form in 1964 I had been offered a place at Ormskirk Teacher Training College near Liverpool in Lancashire; but in fact I went to Birmingham University in October 1964.

I was always interested in history and geography. History, however, was destroyed for me at school with the endless attention to political and constitutional matters. Like many people I found the social and economic aspects much more interesting; how did ordinary folk live their everyday lives? But geography and how it helped me to understand and explain the countryside was great; when human geography arrived, I think in the sixth form, with its attention to settlements, villages and their fields, town development and so on, I was away. Here were interesting ideas about why settlements had developed where they are, how they had functioned and how the land around them had been worked.

On a return trip from Cornwall in 1963, when I was just seventeen, we stopped at Stonehenge at dusk (**89**). I was impressed and my father suggested I read Atkinson's *Stonehenge* which he had just finished because it explained how the monument was built. I did and was hooked. For the next Christmas I had as presents, Eric Wood's *Collin's Field Guide to Archaeology* and the HMSO *List of Scheduled Ancient Monuments in England and Wales* (hardly a gripping read) and began to visit sites on the edge of Birmingham at weekends and in my holidays (**1**). The first sites I went to were the hillfort at Wychbury near Clent and Halesowen Abbey (**66**). I did sketch plans of each site, kept notes, and read up about them afterwards. Rarely did I ask permission to visit anything, often I did not know whom to ask, so I became and remain an unashamed trespasser, going wherever I want, never of course doing any damage and always ready to explain what I am looking for.

1 *Early days as a fieldworker (clockwise from top left):*
Recording inscribed stones near Cardinham, Cornwall, in August 1969.
Sketch-planning the Three Brothers of Grugwith Burial Chamber, near the Lizard, Cornwall in July 1965.
Drawing the inscribed stone in Llangaffo church, Anglesey, in August 1967.
Sketch-planning the promontory fort at Bosigran, near Land's End, Cornwall in August 1965

2   With Dr Robin Donkin, my tutor, at my graduation at Birmingham University on 8 July 1967

I would like to be able to say that my school, Oldbury Grammar School at Langley in the Black Country, encouraged me, but they did not, with the exception of Miss Firth my geography teacher. My long hair, unkempt appearance and generally anarchic view of the world meant that the teachers regarded me as a nuisance and therefore a golden opportunity to direct my interest, studies and reading in archaeology was lost. It was left to an enthusiastic history teacher in the neighbouring secondary modern school, who ran an archaeology group, to stimulate my interest.

Sometime around 1964 I discovered the CBA (Council for British Archaeology), received the list of excavations they issued then and took myself off to Wall, near Lichfield, each Saturday to dig. Jim Gould, a teacher and great authority on the Lichfield area, ran the excavation. He was a sound (though technically amateur) archaeologist and was very understanding and helpful. I had no idea where the post holes or Roman road surface were that he asked me to clean, but he patiently explained and I and the friend I had gone with (Dennis Wood, now Professor of French at Birmingham University) gradually made progress. I did a small-scale excavation in the middle of Oldbury in 1964 and found medieval pottery, though I really didn't understand what I was doing at the time.

3 Philip Rahtz at Cannington, Somerset in May 1978

My interest was saved, nurtured and developed when I went to Birmingham University in 1964 to read geography with two years' subsidiary archaeology. In my third year I specialised in historical geography which involved a lot of fieldwork. There I met a lot of like-minded souls, and was relieved to find I was not an oddity because I was interested in archaeology (unlike at school) and was mind-boggled at the opportunities to indulge my passion for archaeology which the university provided. I was particularly inspired by the lectures of Robin Donkin, who was also my personal tutor and has remained a friend ever since (**2**). In his course I learned about medieval villages, walled towns and medieval monastic sites. I did not know it then, but Robin is one of the great scholars on the Cistercian order – the white monks. I discovered the library full of all the books I had only vaguely heard of and I went out on excavations at weekends with the Ancient History Department. But mainly I discovered Philip Rahtz (**3**).

Like so many other students I was inspired by Philip. A daunting figure at first, you felt he was interested in you and you learnt a lot from his teaching and the example he set of how to work on sites. He would put up a notice about an excavation on the noticeboard in the Arts Faculty and we would all meet at his rented University house nearby for transport out to whichever site we were going to work on. This was always in his Renault camper van or Land Rover – and always accompanied by Radio 3. I dug at Thelsford, Alcester and Warwick, Bordesley Abbey and Badby in Northamptonshire. Once, while digging at Warwick, sheltering in the Land Rover in the rain, he said I was

*4   Teaching with
Trevor Rowley around
1982*

good at this archaeology and should stick at it. Looking back I can see now that this was about the time I realised that this was what I really wanted to do. I would have been about 19.

My interests developed, however, in field archaeology and the evolutions of the landscape rather than excavation. I was asked by Trevor Rowley (**4**), whom I had got to know digging the Roman forts of Metchley (actually on the University of Birmingham campus though largely ignored by the staff there), to do an earthwork survey of Bordesley Abbey by Redditch (**67**). Redditch was being developed as a new town for Birmingham overspill at the time and there was a plan to flood the Arrow Valley for an ornamental lake. Our excavations were designed to show that there was a lot of archaeology left in the ground that should not be destroyed: my work was to demonstrate that the earthworks, for over half a mile in the valley, related to how the abbey had exploited and developed the valley in the Middle Ages.

I went on, particularly with James Bond a fellow student at Birmingham and avid fieldworker (**5**), to develop quick sketch mapping to record all the main features of a site. Over several years (1967-70), while doing research at Birmingham, we went all over Worcestershire and Warwickshire, sketch-planning and recording the earthworks of castles, monasteries, deserted villages, moats, fishponds, mills and so on. I had an Austin A35 van from 1967 onwards and I remember on one trip we sketch-planned *eight* deserted villages in Warwickshire in one day.

By 1970 I had met a lot of archaeologists in the Midlands and all were very helpful and encouraging to me. It was a good time to be at Birmingham. Philip Barker was digging at Hen Domen and Wroxeter (as was Graham Webster), Philip Rahtz was digging everywhere, and he had followed on from Trevor Rowley at Bordesley Abbey. Brian Hobley was involved with the Lunt Roman Fort and other sites in Coventry.

My extra-mural career began in 1967-8, when I was 21, when the redoubtable Miss Nicklin, Staff Tutor in Geography, Extra-Mural Department, University of Birmingham (actually one of those tweedy ladies with a bun whose sweetheart had been killed in the First World War), encouraged me and others to undertake extra-mural courses in the Birmingham region. My very first excursion into lecturing however was a weekend course on the industrial archaeology of the Black Country for extra-mural students from Southampton University (under Dr Edwin Course) with my colleague Eric Grant. This course worried me a lot because I was only just getting interested in the rich industrial archaeology of the Midlands and I suffered a lot of asthma, always my problem, in the days before the course took place. Despite this it went well, we learnt a lot, and I was ready for more.

My first evening class was at Tettenhall near Wolverhampton but there were not enough class members to keep it going, so it folded after a week or two. But I loved it and armed with an increasing number of colour slides (I had had a camera since 1963) I went on to give courses in Worcester, Dudley, Warwick, Claverdon, Solihull and elsewhere. Much of this was very good if nerve-racking training. I shared classes with Phil Barker at Worcester and Dudley, each of us attending the venues on alternative evening meetings. He broke his leg however and as he lived in Worcester he did all the classes there while I stayed at Dudley. An inspection of him by an HMI (a government teaching inspector) had been arranged but as he was not there at Dudley I was inspected instead – a daunting ordeal for a new lecturer (I was about 22 at the time).

By 1970 my grant had run out and I should have been looking for a job. Trevor Rowley had gone back to Oxford University in 1969 as the first tutor in Archaeology in the External Studies Department there. He told me of a field officer's job (today this would be a sort of deputy County Archaeologist)

5 With James Bond (who has hardly changed at all) in June 1975

going in the Oxford City and County Museum at Woodstock that he thought I should apply for. With what seems now like very little effort I got the job and moved to Oxfordshire, though I lived in a tent on the site at the Middleton Stoney excavations for the first month or so, much to the consternation of the County Council officials who wanted a 'proper' address for my salary cheque.

In Oxfordshire I worked on one of the first Sites and Monuments Records in the country with Don Benson (**6**), a brilliant innovative thinker who has been much under-appreciated in archaeology. The work involved a lot of fieldwork and field visits and I began doing aerial surveys, to begin with along the line of the M40 motorway which was about to be built. I continued to teach enormous numbers of extra-mural classes. I remember doing four a week for two terms one year in order to get the money together for a mortgage to buy my first house. I was so confused I didn't know what day it was, what I was supposed to be doing and whether I should be in Wallingford, Abingdon, Witney or wherever.

Before buying my first house at Milton under Wychwood, however, I spent an interesting, entertaining and educational two years renting a room in Trevor Rowley's house at Wheatley. Trevor entertained well and, since he was an extra-mural tutor, all sorts of people visited and stayed for dinner. I met a very large number of archaeologists including Barry Cunliffe (**7**) with whom I have stayed in touch ever since and who has kindly been a referee for me for jobs and promotions. These contacts proved very useful when I too became an extra-mural tutor in 1978.

6 With Don Benson at Butser Hill, October 1974

Oxford was a good training ground at that stage in my career. Although I was not a member of the University, I attended lectures there (by William Urry on palaeography and medieval Latin) and knew everyone in the Institute of Archaeology, the Ashmolean Museum and the Baden Powell Institute. I was involved, with Don and Trevor, in all the Committees and archaeological work in the area – the Oxford Archaeological Unit under Tom Hassall, the Upper Thames Archaeological Committee, and the M40 Committee, to name but a few.

After three to four years I fancied a change and applied for the job of first County Archaeologist for Somerset. This was a very different world (based in the county planning department of Somerset County Council). I did not know Somerset at all but over the next five years I had the chance to drive (and indeed fly) over most of it and I loved it. It has become my home and, even though I travel a lot, I still think it is the most interesting and varied county in the country, with the Mendips, Exmoor, the Quantocks and the Somerset Levels.

At Taunton they were not sure what to do with their first County Archaeologist so I began compiling the Sites and Monuments Record and advising on planning matters which would affect archaeological sites. I determined to see and visit as many of the sites as possible on the ground (I still believe this is the only way to properly understand an area and be able to speak authoritatively about the sites) and I spent many happy hours visiting monuments taking pictures. I began to teach extra-mural classes in the evenings and at weekends for Peter Fowler at the University of Bristol. As I lived in Taunton I was useful to the department for its teaching in west Somerset, which

7 *With Barry Cunliffe at Le Yaudet, Brittany in July 1999.* Teresa Hall

is a long way from Bristol. I taught classes at Minehead, Dulverton and Bridgwater. I developed a (continuing) relationship with Dillington College at Illminster (a residential adult college) and I offered courses on all periods and aspects of Somerset's archaeology. There was a lot going on: the M5 was being built and sites along its route were being dug by Peter Fowler's people (including David Miles, now English Heritage chief archaeologist). Towns were being developed: Taunton had a series of excavations by Peter Leach and there was work on Ilchester (by Ann Woodward and others). There was also the research on the Somerset Levels where John Coles and Bryony Orme (now Coles) were conducting their world-famous excavations on the timber trackways such as the Sweet Track (**40** & **45**).

By 1978 I was beginning to panic about the job. It was too safe, pensionable and superannuable, so I realised I had to do something else. At the party for Philip Rahtz, when he left Birmingham for York to be the first Professor in Archaeology there, I heard of a temporary post at Oxford as a new tutor in local studies. Despite the uncertainty, the quadrupling of the mortgage and the insecure future, I applied. I got the job. It was the best move I ever made as it enabled me to move into the academic world where I could teach and carry out research.

I moved to Oxford to the External Studies Department as Assistant Tutor in Local Studies, an experimental three-year temporary but full-time post. Not only was I to set up a new programme of local history and local studies courses to compliment the archaeology courses, dayschools and lectures, but

Trevor Rowley was off on sabbatical leave and I was to keep an eye on his courses in archaeology as well. However, the December day in 1978 when we moved into our small house in Headington, Oxford (I was married in 1974) was the closing date for applications for the post of tutor in archaeology in the Extra-Mural Department in the University of Bristol as Peter Fowler was moving on to be Secretary of the English Royal Commission on Historical Monuments. I applied for the position, was interviewed in the spring, and before I had driven back to Oxford, the Director, Geoffrey Cunliffe, was on the phone offering me the job. Thus in 1979, only a year after leaving Taunton, I was back in the West Country with an extra-mural tutor's job at the University of Bristol.

Oxford runs a large number of Summer Schools when the students are on vacation, in association with American Universities and there was the opportunity for internal University Staff to teach on these for extra payment. Even after leaving Oxford, I continued to teach on the Oxford / Berkeley (University of California) Summer School held at Worcester College for ten years (1979-89). This involved living in the college for three weeks, teaching in seminar groups, holding tutorials and conducting field trips across southern England. It was very pleasant living in the eighteenth-century accommodation there – I had a study and two bedrooms, though the loo was miles away. The American students were a mixed lot, from college students, public sector workers like librarians and teachers, to rich or retired characters who wanted 'the Oxford Experience' (which I have never understood but which the University marketed well). I taught Prehistoric Britain, not in anyway one of my specialities, but it meant I kept up to date with the literature and visited the key excavations going on in this period. As part of the course I visited Avebury, Stonehenge (**8**) and the other main prehistoric sites in Wiltshire, the Cotswolds and elsewhere, *each year* (even if we did not go there on the Blind Courses, see below) – something I find very difficult to do now.

We had to dine each night in college at high table along with a selection of the American students (who all had the 'chance' to do this over the three weeks) – this was a formal occasion with at least a jacket and tie for men. When I gave up the summer schools in 1989 that was the last time I wore a suit and tie. The suit, which I had had since I was married in 1974, went off to the Oxfam shop shortly afterwards; in the pocket was the one and only tie I possessed – unfortunately a University of Birmingham tie that my parents had bought for me at my graduation in 1967.

When I started at Bristol in 1979, in many ways the extra-mural tutor's job in archaeology was ideal. You taught in the evenings and at weekends, and sometimes in the daytime (we had a crèche then) and after all the administration (and there was *a lot* of administration) there was time for research. People seemed to value knowledge for its own sake rather than some commodity you had to have to get a job; students *read* a subject for interest and

8   With my American Summer School Students at Stonehenge in July 1989

9   'Stop, look, listen' — with my 'Introduction to Archaeology' Certificate Students at Mudford in Somerset, May 1995

enlightenment. We used to put on up to seventy courses per year and almost every Saturday from October to March there would be up to a hundred people attending lectures by visiting speakers in all aspects of archaeology (**9**). As during my time at Oxford, I met many people in the subject. As I arranged courses covering the whole of archaeology and since I introduced and chaired most sessions, I got to listen to a large number of specialists in all branches of the subject. One of the nicest perks of the job was a free education in the whole subject.

All this was to change in the philistine revolution of the Thatcher years. Firstly grants were cut in 1981, then later on you could only do a course for credits towards a qualification. We had people on our courses with two or three degrees already, but retired or pursuing a subject for interest, who suddenly had to collect credits like green shield stamps. The University did not get the subsidy if we did not jump through these hoops. Ironically the one improvement which many of my students wanted – access to a *part-time* undergraduate degree course with study in the evenings and weekends – is still not available. At Bristol, as elsewhere, I feel very much that we have thrown away the interest and enthusiasm of our part-time students and the dedication of our part-time tutors with the bureaucratic bath-water.

But not all was doom and gloom, and things have certainly progressed on some fronts. In 1981, in the Year of the Disabled, I was invited to give a lecture and conduct a field excursion in Wiltshire for visually handicapped people (**10**). This had been organised by Cyril Jones of Wiltshire Social Services Department whose neighbour, Alison Borthwick, was the assistant county archaeologist. After discussion over the fence they decided to organise an archaeological field week and Roy Canham, the county archaeologist, was roped in to help. I was merely one of a lot of visiting lecturers including Julian Richards, Aubrey Burl, and Tim Darvill.

It was a great success and the dozen or so students, with their sighted guides and in most cases, guide dogs, had a great time clambering all over sites like Avebury, the West Kennett long barrow and Stonehenge, where we had to get special permission to go inside the circle in the evening when the monument was shut to the general public.

Cyril did not feel that Social Services could or should run such courses in future and asked if I would take them over at the University. 1981 was a bad time in extra-mural departments following the first round of government cuts. I had the unenviable task of trying to persuade my head of department, Professor Ted Thomas, that running courses for blind students would be costly but high on kudos. Luckily he said yes and I arranged, eventually, two series of five years each, covering the chronological periods in archaeology – we did early and later prehistory, the Romans, the Anglo-Saxon period and the Middle Ages. Very many visiting lecturers took part in these courses and many of the famous names in archaeology gave up their time to bring their specialist knowledge to fifteen or so students each year. Teaching techniques had to be changed and developed. We didn't use slides with a projector, as is usual in archaeology lectures, but instead, lecturers talked, usually very informally, from between tables arranged around an open space. Diagrams, maps and plans were produced on yellow plastic thermoform sheets (**10**) – at first these were made by us, and then by prisoners in the local prisons. The machine that produced them looked and smelt like a toaster. We borrowed objects from museums and had 'exploding' models of sites made which students could examine.

But the highlight of the courses, and the reason they were different to any others and why they have become so famous in the visually handicapped world, is that we were insistent that we always went out to the places so that the students could examine them first hand. This usually meant walking all over the sites with a lot of shouting between individuals to get ideas of distance and direction. For safety reasons, companionship and to provide virtually a personal tutor, each student had a sighted guide. Initially many of these were my undergraduate and mature students and some are still involved with the courses.

Some sites, like Chedworth Roman villa, were not all accessible, with bits roped off, and we had to get special permission to go in these areas. It became an annual event to visit Stonehenge (**10**) on a summer evening and hence I have a lot of pictures of the monument which would be impossible for most people to get these days. Museums also presented difficulties. While some objects were big enough to be examined, most are in glass cases (or in store) and so again special arrangements had to be made. The high point was probably a visit to Devizes Museum when many of the rare and valuable prehistoric objects were brought out. On this occasion a lady who had been blind since birth exclaimed that she could see the glint of light off a gold object. Another visit was to the Ashmolean Museum, Oxford, when a lot of valuable Anglo-Saxon jewellery and other objects were brought round on a tea trolley.

After these courses my friend Julian Richards (of *Meet the Ancestors* fame) took over and ran a series, which still continues each year on archaeological themes (religion, settlement, ritual and so on) and archaeological materials (wood, cloth, pottery, leather). Over the years many students have stayed with the courses; they have had the opportunity to run through all the periods and themes, examine some amazing objects and visit the cream of the sites which can be reached from Bristol. I, and other archaeologists, have with them had the chance to get really close to sites like Stonehenge and the Roman Baths at Bath.

These courses still continue: the 1999 course was about Churches and Monasteries and, between filming, I gave a lecture on the origins and development of monasticism. There is now a full-time team in the University including visually handicapped and profoundly deaf members of staff. It is all a far cry from the early days when we seemed to fit it in between everything else.

I have now been at Bristol twenty years, as staff tutor in Archaeology (1979-89), then Reader in Landscape Archaeology (1989-96), and now Professor in Landscape Archaeology (1996 onwards, **11**). In 1997 I ceased being staff tutor full time and an admin assistant took over the administration; in 1998 with the increase in my commitment to filming, Channel 4 funded a *Time Team* lecturer to replace me, and my friend and colleague, Mark Corney, took over the organisation, teaching and administration of continuing education courses in Archaeology at Bristol. However, I still teach in the winter months; this

10 *Archaeology courses for the visually-handicapped (clockwise from top left):*
Talking to blind students at the first course in 1981.
Students on a lift platform with Carolyn Heighway at St Oswald's, Gloucester, September 1985.
At Stonehenge with Aubrey Burl, July 1987.
Students looking at thermoform maps of prehistoric sites in Wiltshire, April 1986.
Julian Richards flintworking with Margaret, June 1987 (centre)

11 With Sir John Kingman, vice-chancellor of the University of Bristol, at my inaugural lecture in November 1998. Bob Croft

includes units of some undergraduate courses (in Landscape Archaeology and Monasteries), Certificate courses and MAs in Landscape Archaeology and Local History. I still supervise both full-time and part-time MA and PhD research students, with seven of the latter at the moment. Despite my involvement with the media, I remain essentially a teacher and researcher and I am only really truly content when working with my students.

2 Spreading the word

I have always taken advantage of chances to do radio or television programmes (there is a list in Appendix 1) – they are an extension of extra-mural classes and a great opportunity to reach many more people. While at Oxford I had a long-running radio series, with Andy Wright, on Radio Oxford (**12**). However, it was a chance meeting at Bristol which led ultimately to *Time Team*.

The University of Bristol is next to the BBC West of England headquarters and over the years I had had many BBC lunches with producers, directors and

12 Recording programmes for Radio Oxford with Andy Wright in 1972

13 *Tim Taylor with Phil Harding chopping down a tree. Filming for* Time Signs *in April 1991*

researchers, in which ideas for archaeology programmes were frequently discussed. In the mid to late '80s, however, archaeology on television was at a low ebb. The great *Chronicle* series was over and only Channel 4 had a programme, *Down to Earth,* but this was not watched by many of the public.

One day in June 1988, during one of the courses for visually-handicapped mature students, Tim Taylor came to see me about a programme he was making for Channel 4 on the Roadford Reservoir in Devon. He had been put on to me by Simon Timms the County Archaeologist for Devon. We talked at length and as had happened with so many BBC producers I thought nothing would come of it. But Tim was different and a few months later I was invited down to Devon to begin filming what eventually became a series of four half-hour programmes called *Time Signs*, broadcast in June and July 1991(**13**). Phil Harding was involved in these as well, brought in through me to do some archaeological experimentation with flint-working, pottery and fire lighting.

Tim wanted to show how people had used the valley over the millennia up to the time that the present farmers and their families were being moved out before the flooding for the reservoir began. We looked at the excavations of a deserted settlement with its mill at Hennard, the churches in the valley and the information that could be gained from pollen preserved in peat samples. I dug up part of an old allotment, with the owner nervously hiding behind the

14 With Tim Taylor, producer of Time Team, *in June 1998, discussing the integration of the archaeology with the filming.*
Chris Bennett

beans, to show just what we could find in the topsoil in a village. It was all hard work but good fun and I began to see how much was involved in filming archaeology.

All the while we were making *Time Signs* through 1989 and 1990 we talked about other ways we could get archaeology onto television (**14**). I remarked that I receive letters all the time asking for advice about earthworks, finds or buildings; I also said you could follow any group of archaeologists around and you would get an interesting film. Tim asked how much more could we do with a lot of high-tech equipment and a helicopter. Gradually the ideas emerged for *Time Team*, a term invented by Tim (and which is first recorded in my diary in September 1989, though it must have been mooted earlier than that). The Little Chef on Okehampton By-Pass was where many of the discussions took place. Tim took the ideas to Channel 4. I went a few times but got fed up with the endless discussion – Tim persisted.

Tony Robinson was recommended by me as the presenter for *Time Team*. He had been to Santorini with our Bristol University party in 1986 and we had talked about making some television archaeology with my geologist friend, Peter Hardy (**29**). By November 1989, Tony had been approached about the *Time Team* idea.

Over the next three years the main Team of *Time Team* was put together (**15**). As well as myself, Phil Harding was involved as he had been with *Time Signs*. Phil has spent all his life as a digging archaeologist so he has a lot of field experience. He works for Wessex Archaeology based in Salisbury but he is also a superb flint worker (knapper) (**49**) and seems to be able to make replicas of

15 *(clockwise from top left)*
Tony Robinson,
Carenza Lewis,
Phil Harding,
· *Victor Ambrus,*
Robin Bush

any prehistoric flint tools, weapons or implements. He once made a pair of obsidian (volcanic glass) earrings for my partner.

As well as Phil, I had a 'shopping list' of other experts I thought we needed. We were clearly going to need an historian / archivist to sort our any relevant documents and manuscript sources. Usually people who maintain libraries and record offices are a shy retiring bunch, but Robin Bush is very different. A friend of mine for twenty-five years since I met him as deputy *Victoria County History* editor and county archivist in Somerset, he is a larger than life character, *bon viveur*, thespian and amateur opera singer with a fine (if loud) voice. He was the obvious choice for the programme as he is a well-respected historian who has written many books.

I also wanted a resident environmental archaeologist as a member of the Team but it proved impossible in 1992/3 to find someone who was prepared to explain matters in a straightforward way to the public as many of our visiting scientists and specialists do now. Another essential person was an

16 *My research students who now work on the* Time Team *programmes. From left to right, Pippa Gilbert, Jenni Butterworth, Ian Powlesland, and Kate Haddock, Cirencester, June 1999*

historical illustrator who could make what remains we found and any rough sketches of what we thought they represented into a reconstruction of past life. Tim Taylor knew Victor Ambrus who, as an art student, had fled from Hungary in 1956 and established himself as a well-respected artist with illustrations in three hundred books to his credit, including some written by himself. I think Victor's drawings are superb. He has a very good general knowledge of the historical periods and is able to work quickly and accurately on reconstructions of dress, buildings and the details of everyday life. Some of this can now be achieved with computer graphics but there is really no substitute for the personal input of the artist.

Finally Carenza Lewis was brought in by Tim Taylor after the pilot programme. At that time she was a field surveyor working with the Royal Commission on Historical Monuments for England using air photos and maps in her recording of earthwork sites; she is now a freelance archaeological consultant.

In October 1992, we finally had the OK to make a pilot programme of *Time Team* for Channel 4 at Dorchester-on-Thames in Oxfordshire. We learnt a lot, much was eventually changed, but it was clear that a group of archaeologists (and others) could be dropped into a place to sort out some problems. A first series of four programmes was commissioned in 1993 and now, as I write this, we are at the end of our seventh series with over fifty programmes made so far. My life has changed completely and will probably never be the same again.

17 *Archaeology on* Time Team *in 1999 (clockwise from top left):*
Filming and digging at Birdoswald.
Discussing tactics with Stewart at Cirencester.
Filming the excavation of a cremation burial near Flag Fen.
Phil and Jenni in discussion at Cirencester

Time Team occupies so much of my life that it is difficult to detach myself from it and look at it objectively. It is not the 'real world' and we often remark we wonder what real life is like: we seem to have forgotten. Driving to a new location, finding the hotel, living there for three or four days, filming for three days and then getting home to replenish the shopping, do all the washing (for my fourteen-year-old son, James, and myself), catch up on post and phone calls, doesn't really feel like a normal existence.

18 *All of* Time Team *at Sutton, Herefordshire in October 1999.* Teresa Hall

But we set out to fire the public with enthusiasm for archaeology and to show how exciting and interesting it is. I think we have achieved this with over three million people watching each programme and up to twenty million watching at some time during each series. While *Time Team* is certainly better equipped and has to work much more quickly than 'real' archaeology, there are many aspects of the projects covered in the programme that relate directly to the sort of work most full-time digging archaeologists are engaged in.

There is always an objective which we aim to cover other than, and different to, the making of the film. We usually have a 'research design' which says what we aim to do and how this is to be achieved. Researchers (who include several of my ex-post-graduate students, Pippa Gilbert, Jenni Butterworth and Kate Haddock **16**) have usually spent two to three weeks getting background information for each site: other production people and the director(s) will have talked to landowners, local archaeologists and usually English Heritage (or the equivalent elsewhere).

The Team arrives and spends three days on the site with all the discussions and decisions filmed (**17**). Only three days are spent on filming each programme. Initially this was because we all had 'proper' jobs and with three crews there was an expense component. But now it feels appropriate and it adds some tension to the process for the programme. Since we are in effect carrying out evaluations to see if there is any archaeology there, our approach reflects a lot of normal archaeological work these days. Often this is to answer with a few trenches, the *date*, *extent* and *condition* of archaeological deposits. Is it Roman, does it cover ten hectares, and has it been written off by ploughing? What we do is the same.

About fifty people are involved with the making of each programme (**18**). This includes producer Tim Taylor, production people, and an executive producer, and usually two or three directors. Then there are the crews: normally three camera and sound crews, each of three people, cameraman, assistant and sound man. There is also a gaffer or 'spark' to look after the lighting and wiring, and our own technician, who sets up a local radio communication system (the 'comms') which enables us to talk to each other on portable radios. Most of these have been with us all through the series and so we all know each other well and work together efficiently.

Usually about two months is allowed *after* the filming has been completed for the editing process but the archaeology has to be properly dealt with at the time of filming so we have a lot of backup which you will be familiar with if you have seen the programmes (**19**).

First among these are the survey team of Stewart Ainsworth and Bernard Thomason, now of English Heritage, but formerly of the Royal Commission on Historical Monuments. Stewart is a field ferret, like me, who enjoys looking at maps and air photographs and then going out and locating and interpreting any earthworks and looking at the archaeology of the landscape surroundings. He invariably comes up with something new and often this shifts the direction the programme is going. Bernard on the other hand works quietly away in the background completing the essential task of surveying all that we do onto the Ordnance Survey maps. He locates areas of geophysics, our trenches, and any other surveyed features. This is usually carried out with a GPS system (global positioning by satellite) which uses American military satellites to fix positions on earth. I like the idea of this: using a system set up to put cruise missiles into third-world cities for peaceful archaeological purposes has a real 'swords into plough shares' feel about it.

The geophysical survey team also provides essential backup for the archaeology – indeed many of our decisions about where to dig are entirely determined by geophysical survey results. After a brief flirtation with ground-penetrating radar in 1992 and 1993, we have used Geophysical Surveys of Bradford (GSB) on all the subsequent programmes. This is probably the foremost geophysical outfit in Britain, run by Chris Gaffney and John Gater, who, with their assistants, appear regularly in the programmes. We usually use magnetometry (where features have locally affected the earth's magnetic field) and electrical resistance (where features in the ground such as walls provide resistance to a weak electrical current), but we have used many other machines and methods where there is a particular problem and we feel a different approach is needed. Recently we have used ground-penetrating radar again and the results have been very encouraging.

In our base camp, usually called the 'Incident Room' (often a village hall, farmhouse or occasionally pub or club), we also have the graphics team who plot all the map and survey data, produce reconstructions, usually based on Victor's

19 *More of* Time Team *(clockwise from top left):*
Stewart Ainsworth surveying on Orkney, June 1997.
Bernard Thomason with GPS at Basing, March 1999.
Maya Gavin and Raysin Al-Kubaisi, the current graphics team, July 1999.
John Gater and Chris Gaffney with the resistivity meter at Denia, Spain, October 1999.
Steve Breeze and Sue Francis, the original graphics team, May 1997 (centre)

work, and restore pots and other items 'virtually' on the computer screen, as they would have been. For years Sue Francis and Steve Breeze of Spaceward Graffix did this but now we have Raysan Al-Kubaisi and Maya Gavin.

In most programmes about half a day is set aside for filming from a helicopter (**20**). There are three very good reasons for using a helicopter on

20 *In the helicopter, June 1998.* Chris Bennett

this sort of programme: firstly, it provides a superb platform for filming since the overview can be used in the graphics for reconstructions and to explain the inter-relationships between different points of the site; secondly, the archaeology often makes more sense from the air, or we see something new, as with the cropmarks at Turkdean or the earthworks at Sutton, which really could only be observed and interpreted from the air; and thirdly, I like flying in helicopters. It's almost a condition of my being involved in the programmes – the helicopter was recently described by Tim Taylor, the producer, as 'Mick's favourite toy'.

The format of the programmes evolved very quickly in the first couple of series. We felt we needed specialists to deal with particular periods or aspects of each programme and there are often several at hand and others on the end of the telephone. Over the years a very large number of the archaeologists who work in Britain have been involved with the programme and I, in particular, have been very grateful to have their expertise available.

Two particular aspects stand out. The craftsmen and re-enactors will be discussed under the 'cameo' section of chapter 5 but for many programmes we have had specialists in environmental and other scientific branches of archaeology. Indeed occasionally we have had to set up a field laboratory in order to process and analyse samples taken from a site (**36**).

Bones, and sometimes skeletons, animal and human, turn up – either expected or unannounced. Our main authority for human bones is Margaret Cox from the University of Bournemouth, an expert on osteoarchaeology, but one of our regular diggers, Caroline Barker, is also a paleopathologist, available to advise us when she is not in Bosnia digging for the United Nations (**42**).

Finally, and by no means least because we are so dependent on them, there are the diggers (**16** & **17**). While Carenza usually digs and Phil is our deluxe digger, we now have a small permanent group, the core of a superb digging team. This includes Jenni Butterworth (also a researcher), Mick Worthington (with the long hair and usually called 'Mick the Dig' to distinguish him from me), Ian Powlesland (who also drives the mini-digger), Barney Sloane, who used to work in London, and Katie Hirst, who we met at the Papcastle programme, where she was working for the Carlisle Unit. Katie is now in charge of making sure we complete all our post-excavation obligations for each programme.

Diggers on *Time Team* have to be very special people. We want them to work fast and accurately so they have to have had a lot of field experience, and we need them to perform occasionally when we are filming near their trenches, but we also need to hold up their work, often for an hour or more, while filming takes place. Usually we then want them to make up the lost time with even greater effort. Not all diggers would want to, or be able, to put up with this and it demands people with great patience, strength and fortitude. The diggers work long hours, play hard, drink a lot, but are always there to carry on again on the next occasion.

Time Team is a *very* enjoyable enterprise to be involved in and some really good archaeology has been carried out while making the programmes. Since most of the Team has been the same over the years there is a really good team spirit. Because we stay in the same hotel and drink and eat together (especially at lunch times when the location catering is provided by the superb, if inappropriately named, *Bad Catering*). There is no strict hierarchy and no prima donnas – everyone's contribution and ideas are equally valid, everyone has a part to play in getting the archaeology done right and a film made about it. They are a fine group of people to work with in a co-operative atmosphere which is apparently quite different to that which is normal when other television programmes are being made.

By 1996, however, I felt a bit frustrated with *Time Team*. I was always the number two: Tony always did the pieces to camera, indeed he was the only one who was allowed to talk directly to the audience. So, when the opportunity presented itself to make some films in which I was the presenter and talked to the audience, I took it. This came when an idea was proposed to me to make six half-hour films about landscapes in the West Country by a company called *Epik* – named in jest because it only has two directors, Philip Priestley and Harvey Lilley. Philip had been involved in several series around Somerset with Chris Chapman, a well-known photographer who was a friend and neighbour of Tim Taylor (the *Time Team* producer). Wheels within wheels – it's a small world.

I have spent most of the last twenty-five years in the counties around Bristol: it was the area I covered when I was tutor in archaeology in the Extra-Mural Department of Bristol University, so I am best known in that region. It is a rich landscape with the Cotswolds, Mendips, Exmoor, Salisbury Plain, the Marlborough Downs and the Somerset Levels. The producers asked me to pick six of my favourite areas, a difficult choice as we could have chosen six areas to film each year for ever more.

In the end I chose a variety of sites across the counties starting with the Avebury area in Wiltshire, one of the richest in prehistory in southern England. We filmed in the stone circle, in the museum, on Windmill Hill and at the West Kennet longbarrow. Ros Cleal at the museum, and Gill Swanton who looks after the experimental earthwork on Overton Down, provided local expertise (**21**).

Low Ham in Somerset is a site I have been long associated with and is one of my favourite places. It is the site of two mansions (three if you count the Roman villa) and their gardens. A new survey, which replaced mine, had been made by Rob Wilson-North of the Royal Commission on Historical Monuments, and the producer decided to pitch this as a spaghetti-western style gun fight between the old and the new. It was a bit of fun, did not compromise the archaeological content and we enjoyed doing it; many of my more academic colleagues no doubt were horrified.

I wanted to show the new intertidal archaeology which is being discovered all around the coast. Some of the best is from the Severn Estuary where Derek Upton, a retired steel worker has located many new sites which Martin Bell, from Reading University, and others, have excavated. We filmed in poor weather, on bleak beaches and mud flats, avoiding the deep treacherous quicksands and muds, falling into which is a hazard for this type of archaeology. The Cardiff police lent us their helicopter and the air views of the medieval fish weirs off Minehead were surrealistic, like some abstract paintings.

We also flew over many deserted villages in the Cotswolds visiting some of my favourite sites, Upton, Hawling and Ditchford. We filmed in the snow on some days, particularly with Chris Dyer from Birmingham University; but the sites showed up brilliantly as the snow melted and characteristically I got wildly excited about it all. For this programme and for the one on medieval new towns we were joined by another great influence on my career, Maurice Beresford (**77**), author of two great studies and single-handedly responsible

21 *Scenes from the* Time Traveller *series (clockwise from top left):*
Gill Swanton with the axe-grinding stone on Overton Down, Wiltshire.
Air view of Low Ham with the church and garden earthworks.
Air view of the fish weirs off Minehead.
Filming using a mini-camera (on the pole) at Hawling deserted village with the peasant house foundations showing in the melting snow

for launching much of the post-war research into medieval England (*The Lost Villages of England* 1954 and *New Towns of the Middle Ages* 1967).

The programme about Cheddar included the DNA work which linked the 9000-year-old skeleton of Cheddar Man with the local history teacher Adrian Targett. I was only told of the link that had been established the day before the story broke and, although generally I want publicity for archaeology, I was appalled to see the manner in which the world's press descended on Adrian and his wife (**22**). They took refuge in my home that night to watch the news programmes, including *News at Ten*, as the item was relayed across the world.

We should have started filming *Time Traveller* in 1996, the plan being that I would film odd days for *Epik* between *Time Team* programmes, but in May I broke my leg very badly (**23**) looking for a holy well at Llanfaglan in North

22 Adrian Targett with the press just after he had been told that he was related to the 9000-year-old Cheddar Man, in the Time Traveller *series, February 1997*

Wales and was in plaster for five months (over my fiftieth birthday). Filming was delayed (indeed, I missed a *Time Team* at Govan in Scotland and was in a wheelchair for another two episodes) but we finally started filming in September. I still had my leg in plaster, so I stood in a medieval rubbish pit in an excavation in Wells while I was filmed so that it could not be seen. The delay meant we filmed all over the winter often in wretched weather. The days were short and dark, I found the cold and wet intolerable and the pieces to camera very hard work – talking, thinking, smiling and walking all at the same time was too much. I began to appreciate much more fully the skill and performance of Tony as presenter on *Time Team*.

However, we were finished by the spring of 1997 when I was very much involved with the post-production studio work, editing, and voice-overs. They were broadcast to the HTV region in July and August 1997 as *Time Traveller* and received the largest local audiences for that slot of time – over forty per cent. I was very pleased with them: I still think they are some of the best television I have made.

Surprisingly, with such success and such good viewing figures, and despite many new and exciting ideas being offered, HTV have never shown any inclination to make any more *Time Traveller* programmes. I don't think I shall ever understand how (or whether?) the minds of television commissioning editors work.

With my agenda to interest and excite the public, it is interesting to see some of the effects of *Time Team* over the last five years. Each year Tim Taylor wrote the *Time Team Reports* on the excavations shown in the programmes. I

23 *Confined to a wheelchair with my broken leg at Netheravon, August 1996.* Graham Dixon

edited the reports, added the 'Mix Final Thoughts' piece, and supplied most of the pictures. These were advertised at the end of the programmes on Channel 4 and up to 30,000 copies were sold each year. In the back we drew attention to the Council for British Archaeology, the magazine *Current Archaeology*, the Young Archaeologists' Club and Oxbow Books, the main archaeological book supplier. All of this encouraged people to get involved and follow up their interest in the subject. Subscriptions to *Current Archaeology*, for example, quadrupled to 18,000 in the first five years of *Time Team*.

Following a big survey of viewers of the programme, Channel 4 decided to start a *Time Team* Club in Autumn 1988 and within a few months it had 16,000 members. We regularly get three and a half million viewers, but it transpired that up to twenty million (a third of the population of Britain) have watched the programme at some stage. This explains why Phil, Carenza and myself are

24 *Children in archaeology (clockwise from top left):*
Jake Keen demonstrating shale-turning on a pole-lathe at Cranborne.
Children at a mock excavation at Butser.
Tony with local school children on Sanday, Orkney.
School children visit the excavation of the Amerindian site on Nevis in the Caribbean

recognised everywhere we go, for me an average of three times every time I go to Tesco!

Over the years I have given up to twenty public lectures a year about *Time Team* and have met large numbers of fans of the programme as a result. The feedback has been embarrassingly encouraging. The programme has a great following and is in danger of becoming a cult with the main players being elevated to the status of celebrities like 'soap' stars, a prospect I find very uncomfortable and worrying. We are, after all, just a bunch of archaeologists who happen to be on television.

I have always felt that a most important role for us is to involve children and young people in archaeology (**24**). To misquote the Jesuits – 'get them at seven and you have them for life'. Not only do most children enjoy archaeological sites especially if there are tunnels, burial chambers or spiral staircases and battlements, but they are likely to carry that interest through to adult life, whatever career or employment they choose. As a result they might hopefully remain sympathetic to the subject and particularly to money being spent on it.

To this end I was pleased when Tony Robinson was asked to be the President of the Young Archaeologists' Club, run from the Council for British Archaeology. *Time Team* has a page in the club magazine which comes out four times a year. Originally I was to 'ghost-write' Tony's piece in this, but in fact, Jenni Butterworth, one of my research students, has done the job admirably for the last three years and now Teresa Hall my PA has taken over.

Archaeology is almost unique in being an academic discipline, not only with professional members but with a large part-time following, which also fascinates children. The nearest subjects of equal fascination are geology (fossils and dinosaurs), and natural history (bird-watching and mini-beasts). I know of no young accountants clubs or young middle-managers club. I regularly visit YAC branches, often with Phil, to talk to groups of children, and clubs often visit *Time Team* when it is being filmed.

The Young Archaeologists' Club caters for the 9-16 year-olds and there are also now many more schools and colleges conducting A-level courses in Archaeology. However, it is still not easy for young people to get involved with practical archaeology either at school or, harder still, on an excavation. There are the inevitable site and museum visits for children in school parties but it is difficult for children to *physically* take part in practical archaeology. The good news is that there are an increasing number of centres, such as Butser, Cranborne, and the Peat Moors Centre (see Appendix 2), where practical projects are carried out, but we are still a very long way from the situation in, for example, Denmark, which has several early technology centres where children not only take part in many craft activities such as potting, smithing, house building and so on but live and work on site, at a simple level with no electricity or running water.

3 Landscape archaeology

As we have seen my career in archaeology began, when a schoolboy, with fieldwork. I visited sites in the Midlands from 1964 onwards, always with a sketch pad for mapping and a camera in hand. At university, in my geography course, I specialised in historical geography under Harry Thorpe. This consisted of field visits every Friday to sites in Warwickshire. Usually these were of medieval date; castles, moated sites, fish ponds, monastic sites and deserted medieval villages. As James Bond came along as well this was like having an intensive personal field archaeological course. With James Bond I went on from 1967 to 1970 to survey, usually with sketch plans, large numbers of deserted village, settlement and water-control sites in the West Midlands (**1** & **5**).

Fieldwork came to mean to me all sorts of non-excavation archaeology so that even on excavations I was sent off to look at earthworks or the general landscape, as we shall see. Nowadays I would include in fieldwork everything from field walking, picking up finds and fixing their position on grids and lines, recording earthworks, foundations and stone structures, to recording buildings (houses, churches and standing ruins). There are also now a whole range of geophysical and geochemical techniques which enable us to learn a lot about a site or area without any excavation.

Fieldwork is a very different activity to excavation and archaeological fieldworkers are very different people to excavation directors and their diggers. It is a different sort of archaeology where a lot can be learnt but, inevitably, not the whole story as usually this only emerges when excavation takes place *as well*. It is a much lonelier occupation, often with only two or three people involved in initial survey and it usually takes place at the worst time of the year in this country when the grass is low and the vegetation is not growing. This means of course autumn and winter when it is colder, wetter, windier and darker. No wonder people choose to dig in Greece in the summer. But these very drawbacks can be part of the attractions. Fieldwork is a more contemplative activity; faced with the difficulty of interpreting slight earthwork features and freed from the exhilarating manual labour of excavation with the camaraderie of colleagues, the field worker may wonder at their place in the overall scheme of things. In the end, however, the production of an earthwork plan of a site or a set of plans showing the period by period scatter of finds over an area can give great satisfaction. Often we are seeing for the first time what a site may have been; often obscure features can be understood for the first time ever.

25 With my mother, when I was about 12, standing next to the dentist's Tiger Moth in 1959

Many field archaeologists have discovered how much they can learn by looking at the area under study from the air. I can remember my first flight in a light aeroplane. I was about 12 and I had made a model of a Tiger Moth painted in the colours of the aircraft owned by my dentist. I gave it to him and he was so pleased he took me for a flight in it (**25**). It was over the Black Country from Wolverhampton but I don't remember exactly where we went as I was so excited about being in an aeroplane.

When I worked in Oxfordshire I began to fly regularly, always with a camera and always looking for sites and trying to get them into some sort of context. The view from the air is still an unfamiliar sight for most people. But for an archaeologist it is the best way to appreciate the whole site, relate all its features and see it in its context in the local landscape. When the light or vegetation conditions are also helpful, the air view can contribute new information and understanding to almost any site. I realised this early on, from my geographical background, and from 1970 onwards have take *every* opportunity to get into the air.

I'm fanatical about flying in any form (balloons, light aeroplanes, micro-lights and helicopters) but I still don't see how aeroplanes stay up in the air. I know about the physics, but when I am sitting in a helicopter full of a heavy camera crew and me, and I see the skids lift off the grass, I still think it is a modern miracle. Add to this the amazing fact that helicopters can stop in mid-air when you ask the pilot to, the incredulity is total.

Usually however I have flown in small single-engine aeroplanes, wherever possible with high wings so that there is an uninterrupted view of the ground. Often the pilots have been local amateur pilots, keeping up their flying hours and practice at taking off and landing. I flew for a year or so with an undertaker from Wellington in Somerset who fitted me in between funerals. I did, however, fly for several years with a Hercules pilot from RAF Lyneham. Mike Crimble was an amazing pilot with his own mini airforce. He had a Piper Cub which we used with a window modified so that I could easily photograph through it, an Auster in bits in his garage and an odd American aeroplane called a 'Quicky' which he had brought back from America in an RAF Hercules transport aeroplane. Over two years or so we went all over the West Country photographing sites from the air – the Cotswolds, Salisbury Plain, Somerset Levels, Mendips. He was always looking for landing sites in case of emergencies but over the months he learned more and more to recognise field monuments. One day he remarked on a site at Hornblotton in Somerset which I didn't see at first. Indeed there was the remains of a circular enclosure – but what Mike had seen was the grass landing-strip across the middle.

Apart from the overall context of a site which is so apparent from above, why is flying and in particular aerial photography so important to archaeologists? Primarily it is because some sites show up only from the air so their existence may not be suspected before the circumstances of a light aeroplane, available pilot, right weather or crop conditions, archaeologist and camera all come together.

Two main conditions need to be fulfilled. Sites which exist as earthworks, where there are still bumps, lumps, hollows and ditches on the surface will not be at all clear, on the ground or from the air, in dull weather or when the sun is high overhead (**26**). However, in low sunlight, either in morning or evening in the summer, or more or less all day in the depth of winter, such earthworks will show up on the ground, but particularly well from the air as the sun highlights one side of the earthworks while the other side is thrown into deep shadow. In such intense low sun apparently formless sets of earthworks at ground level can show clearly from the air as, for example, a deserted village site. The same effect can be seen in the melting of a light dusting of snow or frost.

This technique, now widely employed, was developed, if not initiated, by Professor Kenneth St Joseph who built up the great Cambridge University Air Photo Collection. Almost every obvious earthwork, barrow, hillfort, castle but especially deserted medieval villages, probably has a photo by St Joseph in Cambridge. These can be examined and copies ordered for the area of any study we might undertake.

Another source with similar evidence is the great collection of around two million pictures taken by RAF squadrons at the end of the Second World War

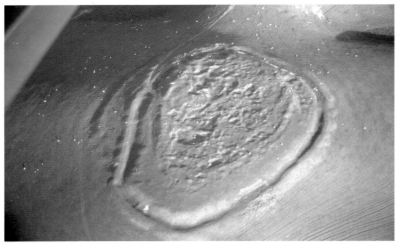

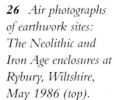

26 *Air photographs of earthwork sites: The Neolithic and Iron Age enclosures at Rybury, Wiltshire, May 1986 (top).*

Parchmarks from the air of the deserted settlement at Ramspits, Somerset, May 1990 (middle).

More or less the same view of Ramspits with drifting, melting snow showing up the earthworks, February 1991 (bottom)

from 1944 to 1948. I discovered these early on and used to go through them for Somerset at Prince Consort House on the Embankment in London. At that time the government department 'looking after' them was regularly throwing them out; now they are carefully housed and conserved in the National Records Centre at Swindon, where, again, copies can be ordered. Many of these RAF pictures show amazing sites and complete landscapes of earthworks. We are told much was destroyed in the plough-up campaign in the war but these pictures show that this was not the case in many regions. The damage was done by deep-ploughing in the 1960s when so much field archaeology was written off, a mere generation before it might have been highly valued.

Sites surviving in grass but which are unclear may show their true character rather better in times of drought (**26**). Even buried hidden features may show up then as parching intensifies and grass over walls, roads and structures dies back but other areas remain green. Many features have been recognised from the air in such conditions during dry, hot summers, perhaps some of the most spectacular being completely abandoned and unsuspected early garden schemes around great houses.

Such drying out, however, provides the second set of ideal conditions (**27**). This is best shown as crops ripen and the phenomenon of cropmarks is seen from the air. This works best with fine grain crops such as cereals growing over well-drained subsoils such as gravel, sands or chalk, though I have even seen it in crops of cabbages and peas. Any parts of the crop growing over deeper soil-filled ditches or post holes, not visible as features on the surface, will tend to grow taller than the rest of the crop as it is drawing on a greater depth of moisture and plant nutrients. In dry conditions these parts of the crop will tend to remain greener than the rest of the crop, again because of the reservoir of moisture in the deeper soil.

The opposite effect will be seen where there are buried stone foundations of, for example, Roman villa walls or Roman roads. Here, as in parching, the crop will be withered and may well ripen and change colour earlier than the rest of the crop.

The recognition and recording of cropmarks over wide areas of the country, and especially in the major river valleys of the Thames, Severn, Trent, Avon, Nene, and Ouse has revolutionised our ideas of how long and intensively these areas were used in earlier times. These valleys were not boggy forest-filled wildernesses but the intensively settled and farmed areas of the countryside. There is little left of the sites on the surface as later farmers have also farmed these areas intensively and most traces of earlier settlements have been ploughed out. These cropmarks are the ghosts of earlier farming, settlement and ritual activity.

The recognition of vast areas of cropmarks leads on to the subject closest to my heart, landscape archaeology. Not only can individual field archaeological

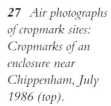

27 *Air photographs of cropmark sites: Cropmarks of an enclosure near Chippenham, July 1986 (top).*

Cropmarks of a probable hillfort near Somerton, May 1990 (middle).

Cropmark of ring ditches near Somerton, May 1990 (bottom)

monuments be seen as cropmarks, such as ploughed-out barrows, henges, settlements, villas or Saxon house sites or burials, but we can get something of a picture of the whole countryside. Between these sites can be seen the field boundaries of the arable and pasture plots, and roads defined by ditches running between the various areas of settlement and ritual activity. In other words, we can often see the various *archaeological landscapes* from these air photographs.

Landscape archaeology then is different from conventional archaeology. It has a lot of my original training in the geographical approach in it, as it seeks to define and explain the individual sites in their *setting* and to show the rest of the contemporary features as background noise. As the landscape is continually modified by farmers and others there will often be a sequence of landscapes of, for example, early prehistory, later prehistory, Roman, Saxon and medieval, and modern. In each generation some of the earlier landscape will be retained and much removed. Features such as a bit of road or an alignment of hedge will remain as relict features from an earlier period influencing a later one. The landscape will be a 'palimpsest' – a word denoting the reuse of a medieval brass memorial, and encapsulating the idea of the continuous *use* and *reuse* of an area, each use leaving slight traces behind.

The tools and techniques of the landscape archaeologist are much more varied than those of the conventional archaeologist. While all of us would agree that a good range of early and modern maps, good series of air photos as discussed already, and a full range of documentary sources and historical documents are almost essential if any progress is to be made, other aspects may be especially important. Good recording of field evidence in the form of either earthworks or extensive areas of finds, is essential but so is some knowledge of early buildings, vegetation history, geology and recent and modern farming activities.

Almost anything may help to identify particular periods of activity or help to explain why a particular landscape looks like it does and how it came into existence. Ultimately the approach owes its origin to William Hoskins who wrote in (the now outdated but very fine and inspirational) *The Making of the English Landscape* (p.14): 'The English landscape itself, to those who know how to read it aright, is the richest historical record we possess.'

Such landscape work is very difficult. You have to be a bit of a polymath and dabble in lots of related disciplines. Some of the questions which seem so easy and you would think would not be a problem to sort out, turn out to be very difficult to answer indeed. Such as, when were particular settlements, whether village, hamlets or farmsteads, created? And when did people first decide to settle here? Documents may suggest the time of Domesday Book in 1086, place-name form may suggest somewhat earlier, but archaeology may show some sort of occupation over thousands of years. Even so, the question of how the particular *shape* of the settlement was formed and developed is equally difficult. When did villages with greens start; why are some villages such a maze, why others so regular? Does it matter if we know this anyway? Well, yes, if we are to plan properly and conserve the character of these places where the majority of ordinary people lived in the past.

Whenever such places started, the farmers in them had to organise the land around so as to produce enough food to support themselves. There are many ways of doing this, and the one that is most familiar to us today – a farm with its surrounding fields, enclosed with hedges, walls and barbed wire – is only one of many. One of the most fascinating if difficult jobs is to try to work out how old the pattern of fields is across an area. It's not such a problem when they are the result of enclosure of waste or common fields in the eighteenth and nineteenth centuries, but how can we be sure of anything earlier?

Counting woody species in hedges, so-called hedge-dating, seemed to offer an answer some years ago. It was an idea put forward by Hooper, and Hoskins embraced the idea enthusiastically. Further work as might be expected, has shown great complexity. Wily farmers in earlier times dug up all sorts of stuff in some areas and hedges often began life with a dozen species.

I have always been sceptical of the idea, so over the last fifteen years I have planted three hedges at my house with a large number of native species in them. These include oak, ash, elm, hornbeam, whitebeam, maple, hawthorn, blackthorn, dogwood, elder, alder, guelder rose, wayfaringtree, spindle, small-leaved lime, and wild service (the last a very rare tree). This would make my hedge at least Roman in date and my 1960s' bungalow, therefore, must be sitting in the middle of a Roman hedged enclosure!

Landscape research also addresses the problem of communications: how old are the roads, lanes and tracks. There is probably more rubbish written about this than anything else. It has been too easy for elderly gentlemen sitting in front of the fire in the winter months perusing OS 1" maps, with a thick pencil, to invent Roman roads, prehistoric ridgeways, and so on. We are a victim of our climate and well produced maps.

Recently those engaged in landscape archaeology research have drawn attention to the landscapes of a non-utilitarian nature. Certainly the existence of almost 'ritual' landscapes, crowded with barrows around stone circles, henges, cursus, and so on, has always been acknowledged, but some would now suggest that even tracts of apparently functional fields and settlements probably have some spiritual dimension to them. This is a very difficult thing to prove but such ideas, often emanating from prehistorians, can make us look at landscapes in a new and illuminating way.

Over the years I have been in involved in many landscape archaeology projects. These began as spin-offs from excavations I was somehow involved in, but gradually I acquired a reputation as a non-digging archaeologist who would look at the surroundings of a site being excavated and attempt to put it into some sort of landscape context.

While working on excavations from Birmingham, I usually spent most of my time surveying and planning rather than digging. I was normally sought out to do the site planning and/or the adjacent earthworks as part of a landscape survey. Thus when Trevor Rowley was digging at the Cistercian Abbey at Bordesley near Redditch in Worcestershire, I not only surveyed the huge area of earthworks, still one of the projects I am most proud of, but also worked out what could have happened in the valley of the Arrow river after the abbey took over the area (**67**). I suggested that the river had been moved, canalised along the valley side, so that the floor of the valley could be developed for a variety of purposes; fishponds, an industrial mill site and water meadows. Subsequent research by my colleague Grenville Astill of Reading University showed, by excavation, that this was the case – I had worked it out from the contours and the earthworks.

Trevor subsequently went on to dig at the Roman and medieval site at Middleton Stoney in Oxfordshire. It was an extraordinary site. We took the turf off the bailey of a Norman motte and bailey castle and there was a perfectly preserved Roman building. It was an interesting question whether the medieval people knew it was there or not. Again I surveyed the earthworks and then looked at how all this fitted into the local landscape. At the same time, in the 1970s, Philip Rahtz was engaged in a project at Deerhurst in Gloucestershire (**28**), with Harold Taylor and Lawrence Butler. Harold, the famous scholar of Anglo-Saxon architecture, was meticulously recording every stone, piece of sculpture and door and window opening of the main Saxon church of St Mary at Deerhurst. Philip was in charge of excavations, particularly the east end of the church where we thought there might be a crypt. I was asked to look at the earthworks to put the site into some sort of context and see if there was anything left of the contemporary Anglo-Saxon landscape to go with the two Anglo-Saxon churches at Deerhurst. Looking back it was probably an impossible task, though I did learn a lot about the medieval ridge and furrow, and of the common fields, holloways and buildings from the later periods.

Once at Hen Domen, a motte and bailey castle being excavated by Philip Barker (and Bob Higham) on the Welsh Border, I ended up digging for a few hours. Philip Barker, one of the best-known practitioners of meticulous excavation, was away for a while and one of his sons, Peter, acting as site supervisor, set me to work cleaning an area. On his return, Philip, irritated and amused, ordered me out of the trench and into the fields with something like, 'What's he doing digging – get out into the fields and sort out the earthworks and the landscape'. The result was a contribution to the hamlets and field systems of the pre-castle period, still evident in the fields adjacent to the castle.

Between 1964 and 1967 I spent my holidays in west Cornwall so, when I had to do a project and dissertation as part of my degree, I chose to study the development of settlement in the West Penwith peninsula near Land's End.

28 *Working on the project at Deerhurst in July 1973. Philip Rahtz is on the left; the students are being addressed by Dr Harold Taylor*

Looking back, this was a good introduction to landscape archaeology. There were sites of all periods from the Bronze Age to the present day, but not only sites, the fields, areas of open country and much of the road pattern was also there. Developments and changes over three thousand years could still be seen as monuments on the surface, and it was all so densely packed that you could walk, all day, for days, from monuments of one period to another.

The landscape approach can be applied to anywhere on earth where humans have lived and modified their surroundings. It is a British invention we can be proud of, but it has been slow to catch on elsewhere in Europe and America.

For example, since 1978 I have been lucky enough to go to Greece, almost annually, helping to run study tours with my colleague Peter Hardy (**29**). We have been mainly to Santorini (or Thera) a volcanic island in the Aegean – believed to be the site of Atlantis by many people – but we have also been to Athens, Crete, Melos, and some of the Cycladic Islands. Except for some fieldwork on Santorini I have not done any archaeological work in Greece, though I have visited many of the famous sites. Santorini, however, holds a special fascination and interest for me because of the association of archaeology and recent geological events and the dramatic change in the landscape. Even more spectacularly than Mount Vesuvius and Pompeii, the

29 *With Peter Hardy on Santorini, Greece, at the third International Thera Conference in September 1989.* Carinne Allinson

volcano on the island blew up (probably in 1628BC) and buried the Bronze Age Society there in pumice and ash. The site at Akrotiri, excavated since the 1960s, has two- and three-storey surviving Bronze Age houses preserved in the pumice (**30**). It is a very moving experience to walk through the streets of a Bronze Age town, looking into windows and viewing the clear evidence of the earthquakes and eruption: the 'bombs', pumice fall, cracked stone stair cases and collapsed roofs and floors within the buildings.

All over the island where the overlying pumice layer has been removed by quarrying or cut into there is the possibility of locating the pre-eruption Bronze Age landscape with finds of pottery and obsidian (volcanic glass) blades. However, only at one site did we ever find walls of a Bronze Age settlement (probably a farmstead) covered in pumice. Research over the last twenty years is now clearly showing the original shape of the island and its landscape and how this was drastically modified after the eruption, giving rise to perfectly plausible evidence that Santorini was indeed the place Plato was thinking of when he wrote about the end of Atlantis. I wish I knew Greek and Greece better; only in 1998 (and again in 1999 where I am writing some of this at Bali in Crete) did I finally visit Greece on holiday.

Also from the Bronze Age but a very different, and to my mind, much more interesting landscape, is Dartmoor. I find most of the uplands of Britain of great interest since so much usually survives of earlier human activity, from early prehistoric burial mounds to more recent industrial remains. These are

30 Talking to students at the West House in the preserved Bronze Age Akrotiri site, Santorini, Greece, May 1985. Peter Hardy

landscapes where each generation has added sites with very little removal of earlier evidence. The Pennines, North York moors and Wales all have good landscapes, but on Dartmoor there is exceptionally clear evidence of Bronze Age settlements, roads and fields, all dispersed within a surviving pattern of land boundaries, the reaves. You can walk along Bronze Age roads and lanes between fields, and visit the various round houses still intact with doorways and bed places but minus their roofs, in walled pounds such as those at Kes Tor, near Trowlesworthy and Grimspound, or scattered among fields such as those near Corndon Tor and Yar Tor. Out on the more open moorland, which was unenclosed in the Bronze Age, the ceremonial and burial monuments of the period survive; the stone circles, stone rows, barrows and cists. It is a unique landscape – where else in Europe can you visit a three-to-four-

31 *The Gallarus Oratory on the Dingle Peninsula, Kerry, Ireland*

thousand year-old landscape, preserved to such an extent? Only a little medieval settlement and later industrial activity, mainly tin-mining and the stone quarrying, has disturbed this early scene.

The limestone uplands of the Cotswolds, Mendips and Peak District also have much of interest. I visit the Mendips a lot but the Peak District is more impressive. Again the juxtaposition of prehistoric and medieval sites and landscapes, overlain with industrial activity, particularly mining for lead, and all tidied up with eighteenth- and nineteenth-century enclosure, provides endless opportunity to view the struggle of earlier people to make a living from a difficult environment. At Roystone Grange recent research has shown field walls and enclosure going back to the Neolithic period (*c* 3000 BC) with later prehistoric, Roman and medieval walls (it has a monastic grange farm), all added to the basic framework. There has clearly been farming here for thousands of years.

In Ireland, three of my favourite areas are also upland landscapes. The Dingle peninsula in County Kerry has a wealth of early hermit sites and monasteries. In the west in particular, it could be described as a monastic landscape, with famous sites like the Gallarus Oratory (**31**) and Reask mixed up with more ruined early churches, enclosures and burial grounds and the impressive monastic site of Kilmalkedar all below Brendon Mountain. This is the country of the great St Brendan the Navigator who, many of us believe, reached north America long before Columbus.

32 View over the landscape of the Burren, Clare, Ireland. In the centre is the site of the early monastery of Oughtmama

To the north, the Burren in Clare is a bleak limestone upland with spectacular geology and vegetation (**32**). Again, there are spectacular monasteries and early churches at Kilmacduagh, Temple Cronan, Corcomroe and Oughtmama, but it is the early stone forts with their contemporary fields, roads and houses which are so spectacular, in places a perfectly preserved early-medieval landscape of AD 400-1000.

North again is Connemara in County Galway. Here, there is little of either prehistoric or early Christian date. Instead it is an empty landscape of abandoned farms and villages (**33**). This is one of the great areas of Ireland for emigration; most of the population has left, a process still taking place this century when Masson Island and Finish Island were abandoned (in the 1950s), and the island of Inishshark (in the 1960s) as people moved to Fountain Hill on the mainland.

Everywhere there are abandoned houses, farmsteads and fields with just a few families remaining, neighbourless, in their cottages. Despite the almost unbelievable beauty of the area, I find it all an immensely sad landscape. The sheer difficulty of making a living from the poor peat-covered and rock-strewn land has almost defeated the population.

The low flat areas of England, are boring to many people: we really don't value them enough and they are seen as only fit for dumping rubbish or building houses all over. But they have a timeless feel to them; I live near the Somerset Levels, which far from being featureless, has world-famous

33 *The Connemara Landscape:*
Inishboffin island off the west coast of Connemara, Galway, Ireland, (top right).
Abandoned cottages and farm buildings, (bottom right).
Deserted village for sale (left). The price was half a million punts. May 1998

evidence for prehistoric wooden structures such as the Sweet Track (**40** & **45**) and the Glastonbury Lake Village. These features are buried, but the surface landscape has evidence in the form of earthworks, for many phases of drainage and enclosure over two millennia as the local people struggled to keep the area free of water so they could farm it and feed themselves (**34**).

It is now known that in the Somerset Levels the first canals and drains were put in by Roman engineers, and new farms seem to have been built on the newly reclaimed land. These and dykes to keep out the sea must have failed at the end of the Roman period as there was a second great phase of drainage begun in late Saxon times which went on intermittently right through to the

34 *Air view of the Somerset clay belt near Brean showing drainage channels, abandoned stream and river courses, and a medieval settlement site (in the centre). Such pictures show just how much effort was put in by early generations of farmers and their families to make this low-lying land usable and productive. January 1980*

1940s when the Huntspill River was built. Much of this activity is documented in the records of Glastonbury Abbey and the bishops of Bath and Wells, but it is still an odd feeling to stand by a ditch and bank (such as Bounds Ditch or the Pilrow Cut) and realise these are features created by medieval people. We should cherish them as much as we do medieval documents, which are usually preserved, but the humble medieval ditch is frequently filled in by the farmer or the house developer.

The Fens must have been like the Levels once but they are now almost entirely ploughed and the earthwork sites destroyed. Cropmarks and field walking (mainly by David Hall) have, however, shown how extensive was occupation at all times in the Fens. His detailed work includes working out earlier natural drainage patterns, as well as the generations of water-control engineering projects which have been applied. As with the Levels it is staggering to contemplate the vast effort, muscle power only, which has been expended on these lowlands to make them usable. We should be more impressed with the efforts of our forebears in these landscapes and look after them rather better, as much as we do with the uplands, where most of our National Parks are.

4 Archaeology and science

It may surprise many people who know me that I have an interest in the science that is now employed so often in modern archaeological practice. I have no scientific background and have never been directly involved in the vast range of techniques that are now available, which enable us to date sites, examine past environments and look at the health and dietary patterns of our ancestors, but I have no doubt as to the great importance and value of science to archaeology.

And yet I was introduced to some of the basic ideas very early on in my career. While at Woodstock I was taken by Don Benson to meet John ('snail') Evans who was working in Buckinghamshire at the time (he is now Professor at Cardiff, University of Wales). By taking a column of soil (**35**) and looking at the snails within it, John was able to say what the landscape was like in the past and how it had altered over time. The snails he studied were not the big brutes who decimate our cabbages and lettuces but minute creatures who are very particular about what sort of site they like – wet or dry, sunny or shady, and so on. They don't roam very far (or very fast for that matter), so they are good indicators of what local conditions were like. As the types of species change, we can see the landscape being altered with clearance for agriculture, or reversion to forest and diagrams are produced to show this. This research has been developed on many sites where good collections of snails can be found, generally in chalk or limestone environments.

Identification of molluscs to ascertain environmental conditions has now become an important part of environmental archaeology (it has been developed by colleagues such as Martin Bell of Reading University and Mike Allen at Wessex Archaeology) but it follows on from other techniques which enable us to understand what the landscape would have looked like in the past.

When I went to Somerset in 1974 I was quickly introduced to the technique of pollen analysis through work on the Somerset Levels. Plants produce vast amounts of pollen, as all know who suffer from hay fever, but most of this, if it does not grow into new plants, rots away. When it falls into lakes or bogs, however, it may be preserved, or pickled, by being waterlogged in an environment where the bacteria and fungi which would rot it down, do not

35 Column of colluvium taken to sample snails at Chinnor, Oxfordshire, (right), and column through peat for pollen sampling on the Somerset Levels (above)

live. It remains to be retrieved by palynolgists, the people who study pollen. They cut a column of peat (**35**) and look at the pollen preserved at different levels (a similar technique to the snail analysis). This reveals the types of plant species as each plant has a differently shaped pollen grain. We can see, therefore, the appearance of the landscape changing through time – at some stages wooded, at others open with weeds, and then regenerated woodland.

These techniques have made us think differently about what the countryside looked like in the past. It is now clear that the *normal* vegetation for Britain is damp deciduous woodland, almost everywhere, including the uplands of Dartmoor, Exmoor, the Pennines and the North York Moors. This was successively cleared by prehistoric and later peoples so that the land could be used for crop growing and pasturing animals. But it was not a one-way process in most areas and the woodland regenerated and was re-cleared several times.

Of related interest, in the sense that microscopes are also used, is the examination of sieved samples from archaeological deposits to retrieve information about the crops being grown and what people were eating. As well as pollen, a wide range of macro (large) fossil fragments such as seeds, pips, leaves and twigs and very small fragments of seed cases, husks, beetle wings and insect parts, are often preserved in pits and ditches on

36 *Environmental archaeology. Temporary laboratories set up for* Time Team *programmes. At Stanton Harcourt, with Russell Coope and Mike Allen, April 1995 (left); and in Somerset with Julie Jones, March 1997 (right)*

archaeological sites. This is my sort of archaeology as it gets us very close to the details of everyday life in the past. Environmental archaeologists examining these can identify the types of wheat grown, the seeds of weeds (arable competitors, Peter Reynolds (**43**) calls them) and the remains of insect pests. Other specimens show us what fruits, nuts and exotic imports were available and eaten. Insects such as dung beetles show us how clean (or otherwise) was the local environment and weevils and other infestations show us the problems of food storage in earlier times before fridges, bottling and tins.

On several *Time Team* programmes we have found it essential to set up an on-site laboratory to look at this sort of evidence (**36**). At Stanton Harcourt, a team, which included Professor Russell Coope looking at insect remains, managed to reconstruct the palaeolithic environment along an early river where mammoth grazed and where early hunters stalked them. At Greylake, where we found a late Bronze Age timber structure and parts of a human skeleton (what had been going on there?), a lab set up in the Peat Moors Visitor Centre Café, allowed Julie Jones and Heather Tinsley to examine

37 *Tony with John Fuller and sample of bones from a deposit at the Amerindian site on Nevis in the Caribbean (left); and a close up of some of the bones which include parrot fish, local rat species and iguana, October 1998 (above)*

enough samples to be able to paint a very full picture of what the vegetation was like at the site in around 900 BC.

On Nevis, a collection of bones from the soil above the beach on an Amerindian site enabled us to get a good idea of some items of the diet of these early hunter-gatherers (**37**). There were many fish represented, including parrot fish and deep water fishes. There was even a bone from an iguana, a creature that lived in the Caribbean then, was widely hunted, and not surprisingly, is now extinct in the area.

As equally impressive as the environmental techniques, have been the advances made in the last fifty years in dating archaeological sites. Most people will have heard of radio-carbon dating but even this has become more sophisticated (**38**). Any living thing has in its makeup a mixture of Carbon 12, 13 and radioactive Carbon 14, and the proportions of these are constant and known. At death, the Carbon 14 begins to breakdown to C12 and C13. It does this at a constant rate so that after 5730 years (its radioactive half-life) only half the C14 is left. Another 50% will go in the next period, and so on. It is, therefore, possible to get a rough idea of how old wood, charcoal, bone and other organic remains are, by measuring the amount of C14 left in them.

The newer atomic mass spectrometer machines, such as the one at Oxford (**38**), can count the number of atoms of Carbon 12, 13 and 14 as they come out of the sample being investigated, so that much more accurate dates can be

38 *The radiocarbon–dating laboratory at Belfast, (top); and the AMS (accelerator mass spectrometry) Laboratory at Oxford, (bottom)*

obtained than previously. The technology is similar to the atom-smashers which exist around the world and are used to help us understand the origin and development of the universe (another of my interests).

Perhaps the greatest dating development during my time in archaeology, however, has been dendrochronology or tree-ring dating (**39**). I remember thinking (and indeed saying in lectures) that this method could never be made to work, but now, as a result of much patient work and some very clever scientists, it has emerged as perhaps the best dating method of all. It is based on the different widths of seasonal or annual growth rings in trees (particularly oak in this country) and the patterns these rings produce over long periods. Trees put on new growth each year, often each season (spring and summer) and the widths of these rings vary according to the amount of rainfall, sunlight, and so on. Over a period, a unique succession of rings builds up into a pattern which can be recognised over wide areas. Dendrochronologists in Europe have built up these patterns so that, mainly for oaks, they have a chronology of ring widths over many thousands of years.

Master chronologies have been constructed from surviving pieces of oak from houses, churches, Roman dockyards, and prehistoric trackways, so that any large piece of preserved timber, provided it has enough preserved tree rings, can be matched against the master chronologies and a date arrived at. Often a precise felling date can be worked out, sometimes the very season indicated. There have been some spectacular dates obtained in this way, including those for trackways and buildings (see Chapter 6), and it is certainly the most precise and secure dating method where it can be applied.

So if we take a timber from a building (actually only a pencil-like core) with its pattern of rings, we can match it against the known pattern of rings (or chronology). If we are lucky enough to have the sapwood, we will be able to get a date close to when the tree was felled; if we have the bark and enough rings we will know the season of the year when the tree was felled. Such a powerful dating tool is almost mind-boggling in what it can tell us. The oak timbers used in the Sweet Track (**40 & 45**), a prehistoric timber trackway in Shapwick, Somerset, for example, have been dated by dendrochronology to the autumn / winter of 3807–6 BC – that is they have the summer growth of 3807 so the trees had finished growing for that year but no spring growth for 3806 so the trees had not begun to put on their new growth for that year. You can almost see the early Neolithic farmers thinking about building a trackway after the harvest of one year and before all the agricultural work of the next year.

With later buildings especially, there seems to have been little use for seasoning. The wood was used green before it had dried out and hardened, so the felling dates must be very close to the dates when the wood was used for construction. So far the technique has worked best in Britain with oak which seems particularly sensitive to its surrounding. But other trees are being

39   *Dendrochronology (clockwise from top left):*
Professor Mike Baillie.
Bog oak sample in the dendrochronology laboratory at Belfast.
Dan Miles taking dendrochronology samples of the Shapwick Manor House roof in 1995, John Dallimore.
The samples themselves which produced a felling date for the oak trees of spring 1489, John Dallimore

40 *Professor John Coles excavating the Sweet Track in Somerset in July 1982. Dendrochronology has shown that the trees for this trackway were felled between the autumn of 3807 and the spring of 3806 BC*

looked at and soon we may well have a chronology for many other types of tree: much *elm* for example was used in early houses.

Of considerable interest is the research by Mike Baillie (**39**) of Queen's University, Belfast, and others, of the narrow-ring events. I met Mike first in 1989 at Santorini in Greece at a conference on the date of the eruption of the volcano there which may have destroyed (or at least badly disrupted) the Minoan civilization and could have given rise to the Atlantis legend. His suggested date of 1627/8 BC for the eruption of the volcano at Santorini was one of his narrow-ring events, the result of a period when the trees were so distressed that they put on next to no growth for several years. What must be happening if oaks are not growing at all? It must be dark, or cold, or both, and dust veils from volcanoes are one cause of this. But other causes include cometary impacts and dust veils from other extra-terrestrial bodies colliding with earth.

41 *Chris Gaffney with the magnetometer at Shapwick, (top left).*
John Gater at Richmond with the resistance meter, (bottom left).
Ground penetrating radar in use at Papcastle in March 1998 (above)

As I write I have just finished Mike Baillie's remarkable book *Exodus to Arthur*, in which he examines the narrow-ring events, which are 2345 BC, 1628 BC, 1159 BC, 207 BC, 44 BC and AD 540, and questions what caused them. Even if he is not right, his work shows how far one archaeological technique can be taken now in an attempt to sort out some of the major events in the past.

As well as these techniques for dating and environmental reconstruction (and there are *many* other techniques available just for these) there is now a bewildering array of scientific methods available to archaeologists for them to employ before, during and after an excavation.

Any archaeologist today would be mad not to use the full range of geophysical and geochemical techniques before an excavation begins (**41**). Magnetometry, using magnetometers which measure variations in the earth's magnetic field, resistance meters which record resistance in the ground to the passage of a weak electric current, and ground-penetrating radar, are all available to try to get as clear a picture as possible of what is beneath the ground before excavation begins. Soil samples can also be taken at varying intervals across the site to see if there are concentrations of phosphates (which indicate concentrations of dung) or heavy metals (which might suggest centres of human activity).

Almost any archaeological feature revealed in an average excavation can be sampled for soil which may have environmental (or economic) information, but pits, ditches, wells and other deep features are most useful. Animal bones can tell us what species were used, how old the animals were when slaughtered and which cuts of meat were consumed on the site and which sent elsewhere, possibly indicating the status of the site. Pottery sherds, which can in theory be dated by thermoluminescence, are now being examined to show where the clay came from, what the source of temper or grog was in the clay, and what was kept or cooked in the pots, some clearly contained dairy products, others soups and stews.

Human remains have always intrigued the public and while skeletons, at least to me, can be boring to excavate, the amount of information that can now be gained from them is enormous (**42**). Certainly using forensic techniques (of great importance to the police and most famously demonstrated by Richard Neave in the series presented by Julian Richards, *Meet the Ancestors*) faces can now be reconstructed with considerable confidence enabling us to see what early people actually looked like. Other forensic archaeologists, and osteoarchaeologists like Dr Margaret Cox, can tell the gender of a skeleton, the approximate age at death, and can find any evidence for diseases, but only of course those that leave traces on bones. There is a whole area of study now, a mixture of archaeology and medicine, looking at the evidence for diseases such as leprosy, arthritis, syphilis and rheumatism in the past.

I find all this fascinating. It is clear that excavation is only a small part of

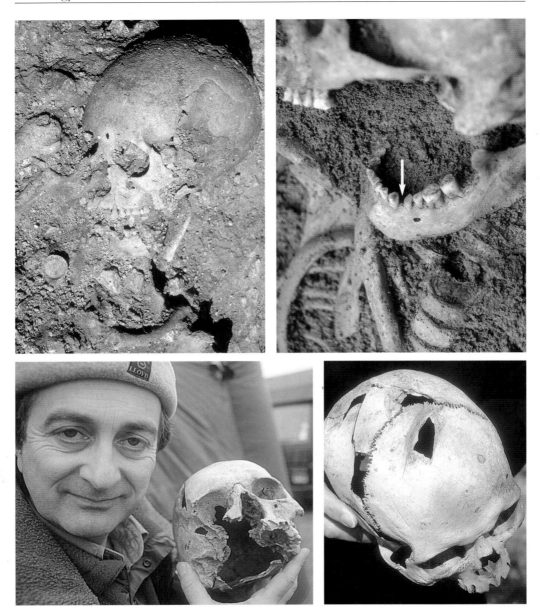

42 *Evidence from burials (clockwise from top left):*
Anglo-Saxon woman with small circular brooch, Winterbourne Gunner.
Skull with facets in teeth from holding a pipe while smoking, Maryland, USA.
Skull with cut marks made by a sword in the seventeenth-century English Civil War, Waddon.
Tony with skull of leper

archaeology as a whole and that one of the archaeologist's prime functions now is to collect samples so that other specialists can extract the information contained within them. Certainly, the archaeologist must be very skilful in his or her dissection of the site and the accurate collection of data about all the features and finds, but increasingly it is the specialists and especially the scientists working in archaeology who really give us the information from the data and enable real knowledge about the past to be retrieved. I often say to parents asking about careers in archaeology for their sons or daughters that it is the related scientific disciplines in use in archaeology which are probably the subjects to develop if they want to become archaeologists.

5 Experimental archaeology and re-enactment groups

During the thirty-five or so years I have been involved in archaeology, experimental archaeology has developed in Britain, though there had been a lot of work in Europe before that, especially in Scandinavia. Experimental archaeology covers a wide range of activities but essentially the idea is to see if processes, which can reasonably be expected to have taken place in the past, result in the sort of remains and archaeology we find on sites. So it encompasses techniques such as flint-working, replicating the implements, blades and waste flakes we find on prehistoric sites, as well as the building of structures and houses based on excavated evidence to *suggest* (and it really is no more than that) what our patterns of post holes and other features *might* have looked like as structures.

Whilst a wide range of low and intermediate technology activities and processes have now been studied, these studies are usually conducted by scholars who are interested in the activity rather than living in the past. However, over the same period there has been the spectacular development of re-enactment groups, not only dressing up in period costume and carrying out replica activities such as fighting with copies of earlier weapons, but also (in particular) to some extent 'living' the part.

As usual, the more conventional stuffy academic archaeologists in some universities have been sniffy about all this activity, insisting that it is impossible to know in such detail how people worked and lived in the past. Certainly the BBC *Living in the Past* experiment, which was filmed some years ago, where several families attempted to live like Iron Age people in a replica settlement in Dorset, probably tells us more about modern sociology than earlier society, but other work has been informative and entertaining.

Some of the earliest experimental archaeology was carried out by John Coles (see **40**) with swords, shields and bows, and by Peter Reynolds who, in a series of spectacular experiments at Butser in Hampshire (**43**), told us more about Iron Age buildings and agriculture than most of the excavations of that period put together. It is a tribute to Peter that virtually all the reconstruction drawings of Iron Age settlements you see in books are based on his work at Butser. Before his experiments with round huts, the reconstructions were shown with a hole in the roof to let the smoke out. He proved that this would

43   The ancient farm at Butser:
Peter Reynolds in a crop of 'prehistoric' wheat, July 1992 (above).
View over the farm and enclosures (top right).
Close-up of the huge round house in the centre of the site, August 1995 (bottom right)

turn the hut into a furnace because of the draught through the door, burning the hut down, and that in reality the smoke would have filtered up through the thatched roof.

Since then a number of other centres have been established – Flag Fen near Peterborough by Francis Pryor and Maisie Taylor, Cranborne in Dorset by Jake Keen, Castell Henllys in Pembrokeshire by Harold Mytum and the 'Celtic Village' near Truro by Jacqui and Imogen Wood (**44**). Near to where I live, the Peat Moors Visitor Centre in the Somerset Levels has replicas of trackways (**45**) and round houses based on the Glastonbury Lake Village excavations (see appendix 2).

44 *Reconstructing early buildings:*
The Celtic Village in its clearing in the valley,
Greenbottom, Cornwall (top).
Jake Keen and helpers thatching a round house
at Cranborne (middle left).
The round granary on four posts at Castell Henllys,
Pembrokeshire (middle right).
The unfinished large round house at Flag Fen
(bottom)

45 *Replica prehistoric trackways at the Peat Moors Visitor Centre, Somerset:*
The Sweet Track based on the track of 3807 / 3806 BC, (left).
The Abbots Way based on the original of around 2500 BC, (right)

As well as reconstructing buildings, most of these centres carry out early technology activities; flint-working, bronze and iron smithing, pottery making and firing, basket weaving (**46**), textile weaving, wood working, milling and food preparation.

We have learnt a huge amount from these activities and the public are generally fascinated by such displays. This is even more so with the re-enactment groups. Today, not only is there someone somewhere who can do or make almost anything that was done in the past, but also there is a group of individuals prepared to re-enact almost any activity or event for any period in the past.

Beginning, I think, with the Sealed Knot (English Civil War) and the Ermin Street Guard (Roman) (**47**) there is now a huge range of re-enactment groups

46 *Most organic materials rot away and are lost to archaeologists but very many objects and structures were made of such materials. This man could make anything from straws (note the bee skep at the back). Woodstock*

covering all periods from the Celts, various Roman army groups, Anglo-Saxons, Vikings, medieval knights, foot soldiers and archers, Civil War groups, and eighteenth-, nineteenth- and twentieth-century army groups. Usually they have women and children followers who cook and keep house.

The people in these groups possess not only great enthusiasm but also considerable knowledge of their period, much of it practical, and they often overlap with the early technology craftspeople. Often they have asked questions and worked out the answers to problems that have not yet even occurred to archaeologists of the period. Those of us who study a period, but from outside it, at a distance, rather than even attempt to 'live' in it (as many re-enacters do), clearly miss something of the nuts and bolts of everyday living.

There are, of course, dangers of trying even slightly to live in the past; not

47 *The Ermin Street Guard, one of the earliest-founded authentic and most successful of the re-enactment groups:*

In a display, the legionnaires charge the crowd led by their centurion, Chris Haines (top right); the finely detailed armour and equipment of the legionary soldiers (middle right); the standard-bearer (bottom left); and one of the impressively accurate catapults, Caerleon, July 1992 (bottom right)

48 *As a musketeer with my matchlock and group of fellow parliamentary soldiers of the English Civil War Society at Basing*

only is our knowledge of the world different but we live in dramatically different social, cultural, economic and technological surroundings. Nevertheless I have learned a lot from these groups and certainly I like their approach and the contribution they make to our understanding of the past. I spent an afternoon as a musketeer with a matchlock gun (which I was taught to fire) (**48**) with the English Civil War Society on the *Time Team* programme at Basing, and the remote and, to me, rather dull events of the seventeenth-century Civil War, suddenly came dramatically alive.

Children generally like *doing* things rather than being told about them; many adults I think feel the same:

> Tell me something and I'll forget it,
> Show me something and I'll remember it,
> Let me do something and I'll understand it.

To this end, from the beginning of *Time Team* we decided to include some sort of practical process and / or re-enactment activity in each programme. This has become known as the 'cameo' when we are filming (although this term is never mentioned in the broadcasts as far as I can remember). Over the years in the fifty plus programmes we have covered a huge range of topics, usually with Phil being the main person involved, since he is the most practical of us. His flint-knapping expertise (**49**) has been used at Stanton Harcourt, Cheddar and Elveden (with John Lord), but we have attempted copper smelting (Mallorca), tin smelting (Boleigh), bronze casting (Flag Fen) (**50**) and iron smelting (Beauport Park) (**51**). We made a medieval sword at Malton and Roman iron spearhead at Birdoswald. Boneworking took place at Orkney, where Carenza attempted to comb Phil's hair with the replica Viking bone comb (**52**). Stone working has included a cross slab (Govan), wall building with flint nodules (Thetford), a Roman altar and a column with base (at Turkdean and Cirencester, respectively).

Building techniques have been explored: at Aston Eyre we built a lime kiln and made lime plaster and mortar; and at Sutton we constructed a small-scale Saxon mortar mixing machine (**53**). However, since wood was always the most important material to early people for both construction and implements, we have had several cameos involving its use: a prehistoric ard or plough was made and used at Kemerton; a section of medieval boat reconstructed at Smallhythe; a section of medieval roof at Plympton; a dark age log boat at Llangorse (**54**); and a prehistoric trackway at Greylake. For a special documentary programme, shown at the end of 1999, we built a full-scale wooden replica of the enigmatic site called 'Seahenge' found in the inter-tidal zone off the Norfolk coast (**55**).

Pottery and other finds figure largely on archaeological sites but surprisingly it was only at Waddon, where we made medieval pottery, and

*49 Phil Harding
knapping a flint hand
axe at Elveden*

Burslem with the Wedgewood factory, that we have made and fired pottery, though we did make a mould for a Roman Samian-ware vessel at Papcastle. Glassmaking into vessels and for windows has taken place at Preston and York (**56**), both Roman examples, and at Coventry, where we produced window glass. Pewter was made at Turkdean, a mosaic at Tockenham, a Saxon bookcover at Hartlepool and the medieval equivalent of a 'bullet-proof jacket' at Finlaggan (**57**).

50 *Casting a bronze axe at Flag Fen (clockwise from top left):*
A Bronze Age axe from the site (note traces of wood remaining from the handle).
Wax model which will have a clay surround, the wax will then be melted out to leave the mould.
The cast bronze axe on the right with air vent and pouring bowl which will be removed. To the left is
part of the baked clay mould in which it was cast.
The furnace on the left, crucible of molten bronze in the centre, and the two clay moulds, one cool and
grey, the other hot with molten bronze

51 Keith Prosser working bone and antler on Sanday (top). The iron smelting furnace at Beauport Park. Filming the tapping of the slag with Phil Harding and Jake Keen (left)

52 *The replica Viking comb being used by Carenza Lewis to comb Phil Harding's hair*

While there have been numerous occasions when one or other of the Team have been dressed up in period clothing, and often our individual craftsmen dress like this, on many programmes we have had re-enactment groups representing a particular period. On some of our Roman programmes, the Ermin Street Guard have performed. At Ribchester, they dug ditches and erected a leather tent, and at Cirencester, using a wooden A-frame, they erected a column section on a base. We had Vikings at York, and Saxons at Bawsey, early-English colonists at Maryland (USA) and Civil War soldiers at Basing where Phil was a pikeman and Robin was on the wrong side as a Royalist general.

Without exception there has always been something in these activities which has made me really think and usually revise my ideas about how things might have been done in the past. I am made to realise how very different (or surprisingly similar) some aspects of life must have been for the ordinary people of the past. This is a very exciting branch of archaeology which will go on developing and making us think for a long time to come.

53 *Using lime plaster at Aston Eyre, (above); and the replica Saxon mortar mixer built at Sutton (left)*

54 *Making the replica Llangorse oak dug-out boat (right); and its successful launch into Llangorse Lake, with Carenza Lewis and Mark Redknap, (below)*

55 *The construction, in October 1999, of a replica of the timber circle (called 'Seahenge' by the press) found off the coast of Norfolk at Holme next the Sea:*
Manoeuvring the oak stump into the circle (top left).
Erecting the upright split oak logs in the foundation trench (top right).
The finished circle from above (bottom)

56 *Replica glass vessel made at the York* Time Team *programme, (left); and the 'medieval' potter at Waddon making a tall jug from local clay on a hand-powered wheel (above)*

57 *Digger 'Rat' wearing the replica aketon at Finlaggan. The linen jacket, padded with sheep's wool, is worn over a chain mail coat*

6 Buildings

Buildings archaeology is a relatively new branch of the subject which interests me a lot. Many people might say, 'But how can there be an archaeology of buildings?' – after all archaeologists study what goes down rather than what stands up. But there is a clear relationship and approach. Much of archaeology is about careful recording and then analysing the results – buildings are no different. We can look at an old wall just as if it was an archaeological section in the ground; we can see which was the earliest piece, what has been added on, and what has been cut into it, like doors and windows. We can often work out which were the last bits to be added as well. We can even appreciate pieces that are now missing.

Traditionally we might have thought that this sort of work was the preserve of the architect – but they don't always think like archaeologists, so archaeological work on buildings has produced some spectacular new results in recent years. Some of the best have concerned churches and this is odd since if there is any group of buildings we could have assumed were understood then it probably would have been churches. Like me, you may well visit historic churches – you pick up the 'ping-pong bat' which tells you about the font, pulpit, altar, and so on, and if you are lucky there may be a plan. I suppose we have always thought that Norman windows or perpendicular doorways or a fourteenth-century tower represented the sum total of the story, but all is not as it seems in churches and we have been sold a very simplistic explanation of them so far. I will return to this later.

One of the earliest pieces of archaeological recording work I did, in the late 1960s, was on a derelict farmstead at Warstone in Frankley parish on the edge of Birmingham and visible from the Frankley service station on the M5 motorway. I was running an extra-mural class at Dudley and someone in the class suggested that we visit the farmstead (**58**) as it was derelict (it was actually lived in by tramps). Once visited we decided to record it in plan and elevation because it seemed to me that it was much older than it looked. How did I know that? Over one end there was a section of timber-framing with brick infill – not something we would expect for the last three hundred or so years. There was also a big vertical timber in the side of the living room and another similar one on the other side of the house in the room above. It began to look

58   *The investigation of Warstone Farm, Frankley, Worcestershire in 1970:*

The front of the farmhouse has few clues that might indicate it is an early building (left).

In the roof space the top of the two cruck blades of the main truss can still be seen with a collar brace. It is all smoke-blackened (below).

The upstairs bedroom has one of the main trusses with the tie beam (cut by the doorway) under the plaster. The timbers are smoke-blackened showing that they were once in an open hall. The roof has been lifted and side walls heightened (above).

The rear view shows some timber framing in the cross-wing (right)

as if the brick parts had replaced or were masking earlier timber-framed sections.

The breakthrough came (literally) when we pulled off the wallpaper and plaster in one of the bedrooms and broke through the upper ceiling into the roof space (it was, after all, a derelict building). Behind these were more timbers – it was clear this had been a cruck-framed house, with one pair of crucks remaining standing on large stones. The timber work was very sound with pegged joints and chamfers on the edges. Much of the wood was black and encrusted with what looked like tar, a sure sign that this had been a great open hall with a central fireplace where smoke escaped up through the roof-space as there were no upper floors then. These were probably inserted in the sixteenth or seventeenth century so the house must have been older. It may have been fifteenth- or sixteenth-century (this was before the days when dendrochronological dating of timbers in buildings became a standard practice).

Once it had been all drawn up it was obvious that this had been a three-part house with central hall, cross-passage with opposing doorways, with a service range at one end which had survived, and probably private rooms at the other which had been rebuilt. Because of the early date of the building we examined the area immediately around and discovered that it had had a moat and fish ponds, almost certainly medieval in date. Sadly, the building is now demolished, though some of the later brick farm buildings remain, so my plans and drawings and photographs (reproduced here) represent the only record.

Subsequently when I moved to Oxfordshire I recorded more buildings: at Stanton Harcourt, Tetworth and Lewknor, and similarly when I went to Somerset. In many areas now there are groups of enthusiasts busily recording the buildings of their region. Often they begin with no building or architectural background but with careful recording and talking to the local experts (who usually started in the same way) their expertise can be developed and much new information added.

The reason this work is so important, and indeed possible, is because of changing fashion. As with much else in life people alter their houses partly to improve the standard of living in them but also to keep up with the (medieval and later) Joneses. So they often have a house which if rather old-fashioned in design or layout but with a bit of refronting in brick or stone (or whatever is the *expensive* local material), and some internal rearrangement of rooms, they hope to pass it off as more up to date. But because it is for fashion they only alter the bits that will be seen and impress – usually the front and the lower floors. Therefore, if you go up into the roof or round the back you can often still find original features remaining which give the real date and layout of the house. This is as true in towns as it is in villages though going round the back and looking over fences may attract the attention of the local constabulary.

59 *The demolition of apparently brick-built eighteenth- or nineteenth-century cottages in Lichfield, revealed previously unsuspected earlier cruck-framed buildings inside, December 1965*

So houses, in particular, can be full of disguised features and I suppose the surprise is that there are *so many* earlier buildings still remaining. Even though many thousands of buildings have now been recorded we can be certain that until someone has been inside all the rest, made a plan, crawled around in the roof space, we will not know how many early buildings remain. Only one thing is certain – you cannot be sure of the origin of a building from the outside (**59**) – and yet this is what was done when the listings (Grade I, II★ and II) were made in the 1960s, '70s and '80s.

Now that we have the powerful tool of dendrochronological dating (**39**) where we can work out the felling dates of the trees used for the main timbers, the race is on to find the oldest domestic inhabited structure in the country. Previously we knew that many houses had been altered in the sixteenth and seventeenth centuries in a process William Hoskins called 'The Great Rebuilding' but we tended to assume that the original buildings themselves were fifteenth-century or so. In fact it now seems that a very large number of buildings from the thirteenth and fourteenth centuries have survived substantially intact. In my parish of Winscombe, in the hamlet of Barton, a farmhouse has been dated to 1278, one of the earliest houses in the country, but watch this space; who knows there may be some eleventh- or twelfth-

60 *Building recording at Shapwick. John Dallimore and Jane Penoyre measure along the wall and up to the roof-line while John Penoyre takes down the measurements*

century cottages still out there, dating from the time of the Norman kings.

If you feel like getting involved in this work remember that it is probably the most delicate and diplomatic fieldwork of all. People are quite reasonably reluctant to let you into their houses to have a poke around – they don't necessarily know that you are not casing the joint to steal the family silver. Also it is amazing how many people do not make the beds or tidy up and they don't want their neighbours or strangers to know about this. A lot of diplomacy helps. I once surveyed a building in Somerset with a group of mature students on a Saturday afternoon, and we had to work around the family who were watching the football on television. This included making a careful plan of each floor, recording the sections and elevations, and looking in detail in the roof and round the back (**60**).

While I have talked here about *early* buildings and in particular *houses* I should point out that it is just as important now to record agricultural and

61 *'This is an original Cheddar Gorge cottage'. Buildings risk being altered so drastically that there is very little left of the original fabric. Archaeological information is lost if recording does not take place before alteration*

industrial buildings right through to the early twentieth century. Many are being or have been drastically altered (**61**) but they all have something to tell us about how people organised their lives.

Medieval churches as stone-built structures present different problems. They are however one of the great delights of England. There may be ten thousand or so left and many people, including myself, would really not like to live anywhere in the world where we could not visit a good medieval church every so often. The one in my village, dedicated to St James the Great, is a splendid medieval example, with a fine Somerset west tower.

There do not seem to be so many good churches in Scotland and Wales where there was not the wealth in the Middle Ages, and the situation is even worse in Ireland where most of the medieval churches are derelict and ivy covered.

It helps to have some idea of the main medieval architectural periods when looking at a church – Saxon, Norman (or Romanesque), Early English, Decorated and Perpendicular – though you *don't* need to be a specialist to enjoy working out how the building has developed. The actual plan and layout of nave, chancel, aisles, transepts, and tower, also offer clues to development as does the degree of ostentation of the carving and stonework.

My colleague, Dr Joe Bettey, taught me to look at churches from three points of view: their site, structure and the fittings attached. Certainly the structure has much to tell when looked at as if it was a piece of archaeology. I suppose the first time I realised this was as a result of the work of Warwick Rodwell at Rivenhall in Essex. He had been looking at what was said to be a nineteenth-century rebuild of a medieval church, but when the plaster was removed from the walls of the chancel a very different story emerged. There were filled-in arches and windows and different area of walling showing that the wall was not a rebuild at all, it had merely been plastered over. It was possible to see additions and alterations over many centuries; indeed the earliest parts were Anglo-Saxon reusing Roman materials. This project showed that you had to be much more careful in saying what had happened to a church in the past. Indeed it was clear that just from the style of a doorway or window, you could *not* date a wall. Just like today, people in the past had punched holes in earlier walls to put in later openings: I have several times done this to my 1960s bungalow, which has 1989/90 windows in new places.

The more you look at churches the more often you see this is the case. A church is a three-dimensional structure (obvious really) and yet one tends to show its development (especially in guide books or on the 'ping-pong bats') as *two* dimensional. The architects who have looked at these buildings in the past have tended to date the walls by the architectural style of the doorways and windows (**62**), but the walls could be and often are much earlier so that there is probably more Anglo-Saxon, and possibly even Roman work about than we previously thought.

If we take a trip to Gloucester to visit St Oswald's priory near the cathedral, we will see a bizarre example which will clearly demonstrate the case. Carolyn Heighway and Richard Bryant excavated the site and studied the standing north wall of the church (**63**). Amazingly when all the stonework was recorded, with every individual stone being drawn, it became clear that the oldest bit of the wall, certainly Anglo-Saxon in date, was at the *top*, above the main arches. Although this sounds silly, the reason is that a complete standing wall has over many generations had arches and doorways cut into it so that only the bit at the top, which would have supported the roof, has remained undisturbed. Just by looking at the date of the various arches, we would gain a very wrong impression of the date and how the building developed.

I enjoy visiting and studying ruined buildings much more than complete structures, and these more than those still in use. While most cathedrals and complete castles are magnificent there is something more interesting (and romantic) about *ruins*. A visit to Tintern Abbey (in Gwent), Rievaulx or Fountains abbeys (in Yorkshire) (**69**), or Furness Abbey (in Cumbria) is generally more satisfying than a complete abbey in France or Germany. The arrested development, the lack of later and modern features and, most

62 *The north nave wall of Studley Church, Warwickshire, showing herringbone masonry of late Saxon/early Norman date, early Norman window (left), late Norman doorway with ashlar masonry above (right) and an inserted decorated window – so what date is the wall?*

importantly, the fact that the ruins don't usually make complete sense, all make the sites much more stimulating to work on.

But I enjoy visiting churches even when not ruined and looking at their structure: there is always the chance of recognising bits of Roman brick and tile built in, pieces of Saxon carving or of realising that the walls of the building are older than was previously thought. Recently looking at a group of early (ie pre-Norman Conquest) monastery sites in the Cotswolds, I went to Withington and Bibury churches (**64**). A case can be made for both of these churches being on the site of early monasteries though there is only clear architectural evidence at Bibury. There the walls of the main Saxon building, with windows, arches and string courses, sit on a foundation of three steps of masonry which must be the Saxon foundations. There are no comparable Saxon architectural features at Withington but the Norman wall with a doorway sits on the same type of three steps of masonry foundations. So even though there are no Saxon features I feel quite confident, because of the *stratigraphical* relationship, that the Saxon foundations at Withington have survived.

Even when there are no puzzles to sort out at a church, you can be sure that

63 *The wall of the church of St Oswald's Priory, Gloucester. Despite the Norman arches, the oldest masonry is the squared-off blocks above the arches, in the centre of the picture*

there will be something of interest; a carved font, often with beasts or Norman carving, a fine wooden screen dating from before the Reformation, a carved seventeenth-century pulpit, or a good late medieval dug-out chest (which my father used to study). Failing all else, some good bits of early sculpture or some grandiose burial monument from the sixteenth, seventeenth or eighteenth century complete with cherubs, bare-breasted maidens or rows of children will make the visit worth while.

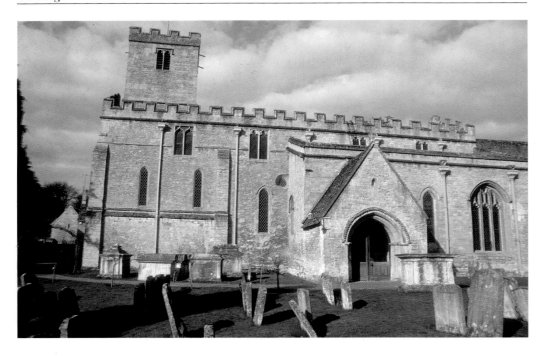

64   *Bibury and Withington churches in the Cotswolds, Gloucestershire:*

Bibury Church. Much of the left-hand end, with the round window, is of Saxon date (top left); below this window can be see the three steps of the Saxon plinth (bottom left).

Withington Church (top right); on the north side of the nave, well left of the Norman doorway, are the three steps of another probable Saxon plinth (bottom right)

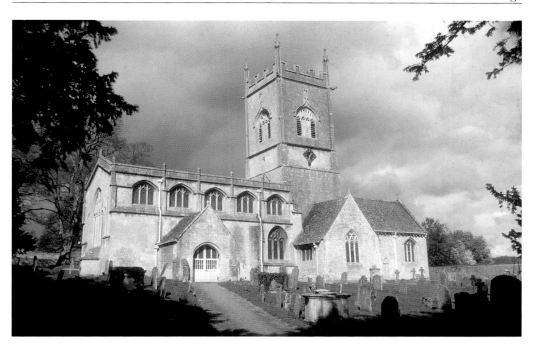

7 Monasteries

Why on earth am I interested in monasteries? When I tell people I have an obsession with monasteries they usually give me a very strange look and begin to back away. So I feel I really ought to offer some explanation of my interest, which ranges over historical and archaeological aspects right through to the present day.

For some of the time I feel I could be a monk, and probably would have been in the Middle Ages. The problem is I don't have any religious beliefs and I certainly couldn't cope with the celibacy. But it's the lifestyle – it is straight-forward, ordered, lacks stress and is so quiet and peaceful. There is also a simplicity and austerity about it which I find very attractive. I'm not really interested in the materialistic, consumer side of modern life (I'm usually thinking of reasons *not* to buy things rather than why I might need them and must have them). There is also the scholarly side of monasticism. Christianity has always been a *literary* religion, it is based on a *book* (the Bible) and so monks have tended to be book worms, interested in research and happy in libraries. I'm like that and always feel comfortable surrounded by books (I doubt if working with the computer and a pile of discs will ever replace that feeling).

So I visit a number of monasteries and have a number of friends in them – but I could never join them and live the life they do. It is a very alien lifestyle to the way most people live today; for most modern people today it is impossible to understand why anyone should deprive themselves of *anything* they might want. Over the years Father Mark Hargreaves and Hildebrand Flint of Prinknash Abbey in Gloucestershire, and Father Bernard and Father Cyril, successively priors of the St Hugh's Charterhouse at Parkminster in Sussex, have provided me with hospitality and enlightenment about the monastic way of life. I owe most however to Father Philip Jebb (**65**), the prior at Downside Abbey near Bath in Somerset, the head house of the English congregation of Benedictines, for hospitality and access to their fabulous library, but most of all for patiently answering what must at times seem to him my weird questions about monastic life.

But all of this has come later. Why did I originally get interested in them?

65 With Philip Jebb at Downside Abbey

While looking at earthwork sites in the Midlands, I had visited many monastic sites, usually because they had fishponds, mills, leats and so on. I sketched the outlines of the claustral ranges of buildings, next to the church and the outline of the precincts, and photographed any surviving buildings, carved stonework or sculpture. James Bond and I looked at many sites in Worcestershire and Warwickshire – Halesowen Abbey, Studley Priory, Pinley Priory, Cookhill Nunnery, Merevale Abbey, Combe Abbey, Stoneleigh Abbey, Kenilworth Priory and Maxstoke Priory, just to name some of them (**66**).

While working on Bordesley Abbey (**67**), I came to realise something of the impact of these institutions on their contemporary landscapes in the Middle Ages. The enclosure of areas for their private precincts, their interference with the natural water systems to supply water, clean drains, drive mills, and fill fish ponds, and their manipulation of their surroundings for their economic ends, all fascinated me. This was a very different side of the religious life from that which had been studied so far: the architecture of their buildings, their artistic achievements and their role as landlords. It was possible through field archaeology and survey, and landscape research to see their imprint on their surroundings as agriculturists, economists and industrialists – and cumulatively their imprint was huge.

I became particularly interested in the development of new orders of monks, canons and friars and their female equivalents in the twelfth and thirteenth centuries. The mother houses of most of these orders are abroad, so I have been able to indulge my passion for France with visits to the original

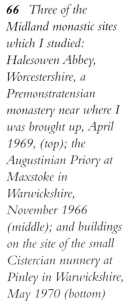

66 *Three of the Midland monastic sites which I studied: Halesowen Abbey, Worcestershire, a Premonstratensian monastery near where I was brought up, April 1969, (top); the Augustinian Priory at Maxstoke in Warwickshire, November 1966 (middle); and buildings on the site of the small Cistercian nunnery at Pinley in Warwickshire, May 1970 (bottom)*

67 *Bordesley Abbey, one of the first monastic sites I worked on. Extensive earthworks remain including, the main fishponds, June 1969 (top), and a number of smaller fishponds, February 1967 (bottom)*

sites of most of these new orders: La Grande Chartreuse in the Alps for the Carthusians; Cîteaux and Clairvaux in Burgundy for the Cistercians; Tiron near Chartres for the Tironensians; Savigny in Normandy for the Savignacs; and Prémontré in Picardy for the Premonstratensians (**68**). Many of these monasteries are also famous for liqueurs (Benedictine, Chartreuse), beers (especially the Trappists and Premonstratensians in the Low Countries) or are situated in wine producing areas (Cîteaux is near Nuits St George in Burgundy for example), so a number of interests can be combined in any study of monasteries.

Great changes took place as these orders were established and large numbers of new monasteries were built – in the case of the Cistercians over 600, over 800 Premonstratensian monasteries and over 300 Charterhouses for the Carthusians. I am a keen European but these monastic orders make our late twentieth-century efforts at pan-Europeanism look puny. Their 'empires' stretched from Portugal to Hungary and Poland, and from Scandinavia to the Mediterranean Islands, and all their inhabitants could converse in the same language – Latin. The fact that they met in general meetings or chapters each year at the mother house of each order meant that ideas could be transmitted from one end of Europe to the other very quickly – not just the religious aspects (architecture, liturgy and spirituality), but also on agricultural, industrial and engineering matters.

Something of a revolution took place with an increase from 40-50 monasteries in the Norman period in England to around 1000 monasteries in Britain by 1300. Many of these sites are the ones we can visit today, looked after by English Heritage, Cadw (Welsh Historic Monuments) and Historic Scotland, and they include some gems, however we measure them, on the European Scale. The most famous are probably those of the Cistercian order, founded at Cîteaux in Burgundy in 1098: Rievaulx, Fountains (**69**) and Byland in Yorkshire; Tintern in Wales; Melrose, Sweetheart and Glenluce in Scotland. But the order which interests me most is the Carthusians, founded by St Bruno at La Grande Chartreuse in the French Alps in 1084. Here the ideal of hermits living in cells (actually little houses) was most successfully combined in a community, so successful that they are still going today much as they were in the Middle Ages, though now with modern lighting and sanitation. There are some twenty-plus houses still in existence around the world including one in the United States and one in Brazil. The only house in Britain now is the nineteenth-century foundation at Parkminster in Sussex; the best-preserved medieval example is at Mount Grace in Yorkshire which is well worth a visit (**70**). It is owned by the National Trust and run by English Heritage. There is a reconstructed cell complete with furniture and equipment, and a medieval garden outside with a replica latrine.

I try to visit Parkminster (**71**) each year to visit the library. To step through the door is in some ways to step back into the Middle Ages, with the monks

68 *The mother houses of some of the orders I have been studying in France: Cîteaux in Burgundy, head of the Cistercian order in the Middle Ages, (top); La Grande Chartreuse in the French Alps where the Carthusians are based, (top middle); Tiron near Chartres, where the Tironensians originated, (bottom middle); and a later mansion on the site of the first house of the Premonstratensians at Prémontré in Picardy, (bottom)*

69   *Two of my favourite abbeys in England: Fountains Abbey, the east range with the later tower (left) and Rievaulx Abbey, the church from the terrace with the claustral buildings beyond (below), Yorkshire*

living in their cells and only rarely coming out to church for services; I always try to stay for vespers in the evening. I am usually given a meal at midday much as it is delivered to the monks in their cells, in a special wooden crate, and invariably I leave having learned a lot.

The Church as an institution in the Middle Ages was immensely powerful and influential and monasteries as a group were an important component of this. If you are interested in the Middle Ages, as I am, it is therefore inevitable that you have to understand the role of monasteries. Many people entered them and spent their whole live there, many more worked for monasteries, at the main sites or out on their lands. It has been estimated that up to twenty per cent of the land in Britain belonged to the Church at sometime in the medieval period.

At many of the sites that are open to the public and can be visited it is possible to get a very good idea of the lives of the monks or nuns who lived in them in the Middle Ages from the layout of the buildings, ruins and foundations. Over the years my family have visited a large number with me ('oh no, dad, not another monastery') and we always try to go round them in the same way: church and choir stalls where the seven services a day were conducted with psalms and Gregorian chant; the night stairs from the first floor dormitory in the east range down which the monks or nuns came in the night to carry out the night office; the east range with the book cupboards, the chapter house (or committee room) where all the administration for the house was carried out; and the dayroom where I like to think of the men or women repairing their clothes and sewing their socks. The cloister was the working area and probably had desks (or carrels) where writing, accounts, book keeping, teaching and so on were carried out. In the south range is the refectory or eating hall together with its pulpit where a text was read out while you ate in silence (it is still the same today in Downside Abbey and many other monasteries), together with kitchen and lavatory (a washing place where you cleaned up before going into the meal). The east range is often the store of the cellarer (or quarter-master), or it may have lay brothers accommodation, or a guest house, or private accommodation for the prior (prioress) or abbot (abbess). All of this can be seen at many sites: Cleeve Abbey in Somerset is particularly good.

Out in the countryside the evidence is equally good. There are plenty of dovecotes (**72**) which belonged to monasteries and where pigeons were 'harvested' for food. The real glories are however the great barns (erroneously called tithe barns or by estate agents tythe (sic) barns). These were the warehouses of the Middle Ages where vast quantities of food was stored, and they show the skill and craftsmanship of the medieval workman at its best. The biggest are enormous – Bradford on Avon and Tisbury in Wiltshire, Great Coxwell in Oxfordshire (**73**), and Abbotsbury in Dorset; two belonging to the Templars can be visited at Cressing in Essex (**74**) and there are other

70 *Mount Grace in Yorkshire, the best-preserved medieval Carthusian house in the British Isles: (from top to bottom) The church; and the reconstructed cell in which one monk lived; Interior of the cell with replica furniture; and the enclosed walled garden at the rear with the pentice leading down to the loo*

71 *The only Carthusian house in England now, Parkminster, in Sussex. Built in the nineteenth century it has a large church (top) and a vast cloister, surrounded by the cells (top middle). Inside a cell (bottom middle) there is a stall for prayers, a bed, a desk and stove. My one meal a day (bottom) (like the monks) arrives in a wooden box, on the right, with tureens of food and a bottle of potent cider produced by the lay brothers*

72 *The dovecote at Monknash in Glamorgan which was part of the grange belonging to the Cistercian abbey of Neath. May 1998.* Teresa Hall

good ones in East Anglia, for example, at Widdington, and in Sussex at Alciston.

All of these monasteries were of course dissolved and most demolished, and their inhabitants pensioned off and dispersed in the decade 1530-40, in an act of privatisation (and vandalism) that makes Margaret Thatcher's government look like a bunch of bungling amateurs. It is again very difficult to imagine the speed and totality of the change in that decade: hundreds of monasteries demolished, thousands of monks, nuns, friars, canons and their lay servants dispossessed, and perhaps up to twenty percent of the land re-granted from the crown to 'nouveau riche' families. All of this was achieved by Thomas Cromwell, the evil genius working for Henry VIII, and it was all done without computers, faxes, e-mails or indeed motorways. It would take as long today just to do the feasibility study and set up the bureaucracy. This was surely the end of the Middle Ages. Many of the families who until recently ruled us from the House of Lords can *only* trace their rise to the aristocracy to the grants of pillaged monastic lands made to them by Henry VIII in the sixteenth century when they were the yuppies of the inflationary Tudor period.

I was so inspired by all this, what still seems to me today to be a fabulous story, that I decided to write a book about it – *Monasteries* (it should have been called 'Monasteries in the Landscape' but I had an argument with the publisher's editor), published by Batsford in 1993. Unlike most other books

73 *Great Coxwell (in Oxon) belonged to the Cistercian abbey of Beaulieu in Hampshire and an extremely fine great barn survives (top); the interior is aisled with great posts supporting a timber roof with stone tiles (below)*

74 *The Knights Templars had two barns at their manor of Cressing in Essex. Above is the Wheat Barn, while left is the interior of the Barley Barn with its forest of timbers*

75 *My current research focuses on early monasteries and I am particularly interested in the Irish sites.*
Examples shown here (clockwise from top left):
Kilmacduagh in Galway with its ruined cathedral and early churches and its complete round tower.
The round tower and one of the superb decorated high crosses at the impressive early monastic site at
Monasterboice in County Louth.
The early high cross, round tower and later church at Dromiskin in County Louth.
The small restored church of St Macdara's island, off the coast of Connemara in Galway

on monasteries I wanted to show that they had had this long 1500 year history, so I dealt with the origins of monasticism in the deserts of Egypt and the Middle East, as well as the revival of monasteries in this country in the late eighteenth century and their survival through to the present day. The early chapters, dealing with the period 500-1100, were difficult to write as there was much less information and a lot less clarity of what a monastery was (rather than just a group of priests or monks).

Since then I have discovered Ireland with its wealth of early monasteries and its different Early Christian history (**75**). So I decided to write what is proving to be a difficult book on early monasteries in the British Isles. Most of my time that is not taken up with filming, the Shapwick Project, or just day to day living is going into the preparation and research for this book, but it will clearly be several years yet before it sees the light of day.

8 Medieval settlements in Somerset and the Shapwick Project

While *Time Team* and other filming has occupied a great deal of my time over the last ten years it has never constituted the whole of my life and other things are sometimes more important. In 1999, along with my co-director Chris Gerrard and many others, I am coming to the end of a ten-year major programme of research at Shapwick in Somerset, a village situated on the Polden Hills between Bridgwater and Glastonbury.

What on earth have I been doing in a Somerset village for over a decade? The answer to this question lies in the study of rural settlements which has been going on vigorously since the end of World War II. It is an interesting and exciting story and in many ways it gets to the heart of what we think of as England because much of the work has been concerned with the English village. The Tourist Boards would like us and foreign visitors to see the village as the normal English (not really British) settlement, with its ancient church, picturesque thatched pub and cottages all arranged around a village green with pond (**76**). They are always picturesque and ancient, and villages always nestle, don't they? This is the image of many calendars and guide books we see for sale and cards we receive each Christmas. It is what I call the 'forever Ambridge' image. It is usually said that villages were created by Anglo-Saxons coming in after the Romans had left – rather as if, as one ferry went out loaded with the Romans, another came in with the Saxons, who all carried in their back pockets planning applications for the nucleated villages they were going to build. The reality has turned out to be very different and much more interesting.

The story begins back in the 1940s when various researchers began to look at the evidence for deserted medieval villages. William Hoskins was involved in this but the greatest researcher was without doubt my friend Professor Maurice Beresford (**77**) from Leeds University. Maurice almost single-handedly developed the national study of deserted medieval villages (DMVs) through the Deserted Medieval Village Research Group (DMVRG) and his book on *The Lost Villages of England* (published in 1954). He was joined by John Hurst and together they excavated part of the deserted village of Wharram Percy in Yorkshire (**78**). Over the forty seasons that this excavation ran several new generations of scholars were trained in settlement

76 *Urchfont, Wiltshire, the archetypal English village. Here, as elsewhere, the church, manor house, village green and duck pond belie a much more complex development*

archaeology. The site is now open to the public and there are several accessible publications. Deserted villages had arrived on the maps of the archaeology of any region, the subject was taught in medieval archaeology courses and undergraduates began to make examination howlers – 'there are only two deserted medieval villages and they are called Beresford and Hurst!'.

Wharram Percy showed us that villages were very different to what we thought and had expected to find. The church seemed to be a fixed point, probably from the eighth or ninth century, but even with that, most of its history, like an iceberg, was hidden, buried in the ground: an important lesson for what we think we know about our medieval parish churches. There were (at least) two manor houses, though one had been abandoned and built over (so it may have been *one* which moved). But the village itself, which may have been deliberately laid out as a planned unit, only began in the ninth or tenth century. Before the village the area had been farmed from a scatter of prehistoric, Roman and then Saxon (or Anglian) centres, one presumably succeeding another. Since the end of the Middle Ages, again the area has been farmed from two or three farmsteads. The village then, had only existed for about 500 years of the last 3000 years, leading John Hurst to describe the

77   *Maurice Beresford (left) and John Hurst (right) at the presentation, at Wharram Percy, of a book in honour of their research into deserted villages. July 1989*

village as an 'aberration' in the settlement of the area. I think we were all surprised by the amount of early (ie prehistoric, Roman and pre-1100) activity there was on the site. In particular much of the village layout, its fields and property boundaries and its lanes, belonged to much earlier periods but had remained (in use?) and influenced the way the medieval village had been organised. We would clearly need to remember this with other villages elsewhere that we might study.

While all this research was going on I had been working in Oxfordshire, where a great deal had been done on DMVs and I was only able to add some shrunken village sites to what was known already. But when I got to Somerset in 1974, I found that very little work had taken place. No one had systematically looked at the county and only twenty or so sites were known. As I had to compile a Sites and Monuments record for the county I set about looking for evidence of shrunken and deserted settlements. It was not difficult to find it. The air photos taken by the RAF in the 1940s showed extensive

78 *Wharram Percy, Yorkshire, the ruined church and the surviving row of cottages, all that remains of the extensive medieval village that exists all around as earthworks*

earthworks in south-east Somerset and although some had been ploughed away when I visited them on the ground, others were very well preserved but totally unknown. It was a funny feeling finding so many sites which had not been previously recognised. The most exciting without doubt was Nether Adber (**79**). An air photograph had been taken by Professor St Joseph of this site in 1966 and it showed clearly on the 1940s RAF air pictures. I first went there in 1976. I called in after going to Richard Bradley's wedding and was amazed while having a wee behind a hedge to see such good earthworks surviving in the field.

After a few years I had several hundred sites listed and mapped, mostly from air photographs, but I had also looked at all the early maps and gone through the easily accessible documentation. However, I had a problem with west Somerset and the Exmoor area where there did not seem to be any deserted village remains. One day I mentioned this to Hilary Binding, one of the local historians. She told me that there was a deserted *farmstead* at Bagley (**80**) (near Dunkery Beacon on the highest part of Exmoor) but she knew of no deserted medieval villages – though there were deserted nineteenth-century industrial villages on the Brendon Hills which had been involved in iron ore working.

This was the lead I needed – there were no deserted villages because there

79 *The deserted village of Nether Adber, Mudford, Somerset:*
View across the site with the last house and pond, (top); one of the well-preserved earthwork house sites, (middle); and air view showing the earthworks of houses, lanes and platforms which probably indicate the farmyards, (bottom)

had never been any medieval villages – but there were deserted farmsteads (and hamlets) because the *normal* settlement pattern in the area had been farmsteads and hamlets in the Middle Ages. I set about looking for deserted farm sites. Again I used the air pictures, but found other useful sources in the first edition Ordnance Survey six inch maps which showed abandoned farm sites and, even better, the tithe maps which gave the names of old farms and showed sites in the 1840s which had subsequently disappeared. Amazingly though the most useful source was a document of 1327 printed by the Somerset Record Society in 1889. This listed all the vills (or 'manors') together with all the inhabitants who were paying the lay subsidy (or tax) to the crown. Many of their surnames recorded trades or were downright rude referring to personal characteristics, but a large proportion were the names of farms and it became clear that the inhabitants were named after the farms they lived in. Here was a quick and easy way to compare the maps of 1840 and later with recorded surnames. Over a space of eighteen months I found dozens of deserted medieval farm sites on and around Exmoor in this way. I went round to see them and again, although some had been destroyed by agricultural improvement, it was exciting to find large numbers of previously unrecognised sites. I was seeing them for the first time for what they were: Mousehanger (**80**) in Winsford where had lived in 1327, William de Mauleshangre; Gupworthy in Brompton Regis, where Mabel de Gopeworthy lived; Slade in Dulverton, where Henry and Roger atte Slade lived. Altogether I added over 100 sites to the record.

The interest generated by Wharram Percy stimulated research elsewhere. Ideas moved on from looking just at *deserted* sites to looking at those villages which were shrunken or indeed which only had small areas of earthworks attached. Other scholars such as Jean Le Patourel, Alan Aberg and James Bond looked at moated sites which often occur in those areas (like Suffolk, Essex and north Worcestershire and Warwickshire) where there never were medieval villages. Yet others like Brian Roberts at Durham began to look at surviving medieval villages (which is actually most of them, perhaps ten to twelve thousand altogether), to see if their sites, where they were built or their layout (or plan), offered any clues to how they had developed. Most of us realised that it was only by looking at *all* settlements (villages, hamlets and farmsteads) including the deserted, shrunken and surviving examples, and also those of Anglo-Saxon, medieval and post-medieval date, that we would really be able to get the full story of settlement in any area. My friend, Chris Taylor, began to do this with his influential book *Village and Farmstead*, published in 1983.

The result of all the work in the 1950s, 1960s and 1970s was that it appeared likely that villages were a relatively late creation in the landscape, of the ninth, tenth and eleventh centuries rather than the fifth or sixth as was previously thought. In many cases they seem to have been planned, or at least deliberately

80 Deserted farm sites in West Somerset: Bagley in Luccombe parish mentioned in Domesday Book in 1086, (top) and Mousehanger in Winsford parish, mentioned in 1327 (bottom)

laid out, or been the result of clusters of buildings in small centres such as those around manors, churches, greens or road junctions being joined together with further, later rows of buildings. Generally it looked as if hamlets or farmsteads had been the 'normal' type of settlement, rather than villages: much of Devon, Cornwall, West Somerset, Wales and the Welsh Border and south-eastern England are still largely areas of farmsteads and hamlets. Villages were only built in certain areas and in some cases their creation had taken place alongside the removal of pre-existing farmsteads scattered over the area and the village. This seemed to me a much more exciting story than the old 'Saxons replace Romans' one but we all wondered why such a dramatic change had taken place and who might have engineered it in late Saxon England.

By the mid-1980s it seemed to me that it would be useful to look at a settlement in the west country where we had a village which might have replaced a group of farmsteads. In 1985, after four years of cuts to continuing education under Thatcher's government, I felt I needed a change; I needed to get back into the field and do some archaeological fieldwork. I resigned from 19 committees, because the same items we had dealt with ten years before began to come round again and I realised as archaeologists we were really powerless to achieve anything without different legislation or greater financial resources. I looked at a number of places in Somerset, my main area of interest, including Cheddar, North and South Petherton and North Curry.

So why did we end up choosing Shapwick? A friend of mine, Nick Corcos, had examined Shapwick for his MA dissertation at Leicester University. He noted that on an eighteenth-century map, that the village appeared to be planned (**81**). More significantly, the furlong names of blocks of peasant strips in the common fields, described in a document of 1515, were names that we would expect to be applied to earlier settlements. In the Middle Ages and later, these furlong areas were arable fields. This was just what I was looking for; a parish where the settlements might have been originally dispersed but which had probably been replaced by a nucleated village.

It took eighteen months to get the project set up. Almost the whole parish was owned by Lord Vestey, who lives in the Cotswolds, so on a notable occasion we met the land agent, Bill Robbins, to discuss access to the land. Bill is a busy man and my colleague Michael Costen and myself had just ten minutes at a meeting on the churchyard wall at Shapwick to convince Bill of our good intentions. Archaeologists often write about the archaeological background to their projects but they rarely tell you about this side of it. Nothing happens without the consent of the landowners and tenants and we were lucky at Shapwick that the land agent and the farmers have always been so helpful and co-operative.

I was pretty sure of what I wanted to do but it was a while before we got started. I knew about all the techniques we should use and what I hoped to find out but again archaeologists rarely tell you that they learn most as they go

81 Air photograph of Shapwick Village from the south. The manor house is top left; the church in the centre

along. Nothing is that predetermined and in the first few years we were all on a steep learning curve. Looking back, the single land-ownership was the greatest help with only half a dozen farmers to deal with. More significant was the attraction of an amazingly diverse group of people who have provided the bulk of the vast amount of free labour needed to carry out the weekly fieldwork and research over a ten year period (**82**). It is invidious to pick out individuals but I am going to anyway (in order of number of lines fieldwalked) – Shirley Everden, Harry Jelley, Dennis Hill-Cottingham, Michael Costen, Teresa Hall, Nick Corcos, John Day, Richard Peglar, Sue Fitton, and Brian Harris.

82   The Shapwick fieldworkers: in the winter on a bitterly cold day in November 1993 (note the VW van) (top); and in Spring 1997 (bottom)

Other factors ensured our success. Chris Gerrard (**83**), formerly one of my research students and a lecturer at King Alfred's College, Winchester, offered to look after the finds and direct *all* the excavations we undertook from 1993 onwards. At the time I don't think I fully appreciated what a fantastic offer this was. Ten years and a quarter of a million finds later, I do. I asked members of the Somerset Vernacular Buildings Research Group, who had already surveyed a sixteenth-century building used as a school in the village, if they

would like to look at the rest of the early buildings (**60**). Again, at the time, I did not fully realise what an important request this was and how significant to the project their findings would be. Generally, I adopted the approach that any individual or group, who had something to research of interest, was welcome to get involved – in no time we had geophysics, botany and geological surveys, buildings survey, maps analysis, study of documents and field walking all under way. The project also formed the basis for a great number of teaching and practical projects including undergraduates and research students, and people on courses for the visually-handicapped (**84**).

Many modern archaeological field projects today claim to be multi-disciplinary with all the different aspects integrated but often it appears that each discipline follows a separate and discreet path. The Shapwick Project was truly interdisciplinary. There was no committee or management structure to it; we had no formal meetings, secretary or minutes. Instead we had endless

84   Above Chris and I talk to the students and others who helped on the excavations each summer, June 1999; and, left, Colin Howard, a visually-handicapped student, surveying parch marks at Shapwick, July 1995

spontaneous discussions, especially when excavations began in 1993, at which we each explained our ideas, hunches, findings and problems. Time and again we learned from colleagues looking at some completely different aspect of the parish.

I emphasise all this because it is not like modern (I suspect largely American-derived) management styles which rest on vast administrative and bureaucratic organisation and which seem to require the answers, and the full costs of getting them, even before work has begun and the problems have been encountered. I was rather more attracted to a scholarly approach with debate and discussion and the evolution of ideas. I suppose I got this from Philip Rahtz and it developed at Wharram Percy over forty years; it still seems to me the best way to make genuine progress in developing our knowledge of the past.

An example from Shapwick will show how the approach worked. At the northern end of the village is the larger of the former manor houses, Shapwick House, a building which has clearly been altered a lot (**85**). But ever since the eighteenth century when the Somerset historian, John Collinson wrote, it has been assumed that this was a new building of the seventeenth century – it has transomed and mullioned windows of that date. Nearby is a moated site, and since we are told in a document of 1515 that the abbot of Glastonbury's manor here was moated, before we examined it we presumed that this was it. When I first saw it, I realised that the island was too small for a manor site for the abbots – after all, the abbey was the richest in the country and the abbots, powerful medieval magnates. When the buildings surveyors looked at Shapwick House, however, they found that it had a basic medieval plan of hall, cross-passage and two wings, but more significantly it had a fine well-preserved medieval roof of twelve trusses which had not previously been recognised.

Dan Miles took samples for dendrochronology (**39**) and gave us a felling date for the oak timbers of spring 1489; the detached medieval kitchen roof timbers were dated similarly to spring 1428. Here was the abbot's manor house, not on the island behind. But if this was the case what about the 1515 document which stated that there was: 'The demesne there with hall, chamber, storeroom, kitchen, stable, garden and barton, *inside la mote*, containing one acre and a half and half a perch…', with 'an oxhouse with barton *outside la mote*'. This seems to say that there was a moat around the present house; we could assume that the barton outside the moat was the great barn shown on the only early prospect of Shapwick – a print of 1791 executed by Bonner for Collinson's book.

A detailed survey by James Bond showed that indeed the moat could still be seen around three sides of the house as a slight earthwork, in places only a few inches deep. When the owner wanted to put underground the main electric cable, Chris and his students dug the trench for him, thereby

85 Multidisciplinary research at Shapwick House (clockwise from top):
The main manor with the detached kitchen with its bell cupola to the left.
Air view of the manor in its park. The moat (mentioned in 1515) ran around the house in the centre.
The park beyond was created when part of the village was cleared by 1791.
Excavation of the medieval moat around the manor in 1997.
The main oak trusses of the roof, dated by dendrochronology to 1489

revealing the edge of the moat with a stone wall, a bridge abutment or gate, and the remains of buildings on the island, one of which may have been an earlier kitchen. A trench dug in a later year showed that the moat was up to four metres deep, 12m wide and had been filled up around 1625 when fashion had changed and gardens around the house were deemed to be more attractive than a soggy smelly medieval ditch. The finds from the infill showed a rich wealthy household – even their rubbish was high class.

While this example shows the variety of techniques and specialists, and the way their individual approaches all interact to produce the story (experts in historic buildings, documentary research, early maps and prints, earthwork survey, excavation and finds analysis), it will be the seemingly endless days of field work in the rain which will remain my enduring memory of the Shapwick Project.

I felt that, if we looked at each field as it was ploughed and harrowed and collected the surface finds of pottery, flint, stone and so on (basic field archaeological technique), we would find the early settlements that may have predated the village. Each Thursday a group of us would meet at the post office (now sadly defunct) and then collect our poles, canes, tapes, plastic bags and maps from the cottage (the estate lent us a succession of derelict cottages to store our equipment and wash and store our finds) and set off to whichever field(s) was available. I, or one of my lieutenants, Sue Fitton and Teresa Hall (**86**), had usually arrived a bit earlier and seen the farmer about the fields we wanted to walk. Like a well-oiled machine the fieldworkers, volunteers of all ages and from all walks of life, would lay out the fields in lines and sections, labels would be written, and put into bags, and these would be dished out. After coffee we would spend two to three hours walking 25m lengths for ten minutes per length, putting finds into our bags. Rows 25m apart are close enough to locate any early sites but just too far away to carry on a conversation; fieldwork is lonely and watching the weather roll in from the west, on cold and bleak November and December days is unforgettable (**87**). It is also an amazing activity in being able quickly to revolutionise our ideas about how people have used an area in the past. Although it is often cold and wet, I love it, and I shall miss the Thursdays at Shapwick with my fieldwalking friends more than I can describe.

The end result was very satisfying: over two thirds of the parish sampled, some 108 fields and the locating of totally new prehistoric sites from flints, Romano-British settlements from pottery and building debris, and extensive areas of medieval and post-medieval finds. Shapwick is probably no different to countless other villages or medieval sites – it has just been looked at much more intensively than most others.

I think we can now say as far as all this evidence allows that there were indeed early medieval farms and hamlets spread across the area of the later parish, places like Enworthy, Sladwick, possibly Abchester, and the area round

‹86 My lieutenants at Shapwick, Sue Fitton (left) and Teresa Hall. When I was not able to be at Shapwick they organised the weekly fieldwork, recording, washing and bagging of finds

the early church, which were replaced by the present village. This may have taken place by the mid-tenth century, though of course, the village plan with all its farms may not have been fully built-up until perhaps the thirteenth and fourteenth centuries.

This all sounds coldly academic. What on earth did the locals think about such a momentous change? After all the move from living in your own farm surrounded by your fields to a place where you had close neighbours and where you were expected to work communally and co-operatively in the new common fields, was one of the most dramatic changes to have happened to the people in the last two thousand years.

In the end I wrote a story about it, to try to sort out my ideas. In it there are the reluctant elderly farmers, the young people who think it is a good idea and the officials who are trying to make the changes happen.

There is so much we would like to know about what such people thought of the changes that affected their lives in the past. Archaeology, and especially my kind of archaeology, still represents our best chance of getting at the story. I have no doubt we are going to learn a very great deal about the lives of such ordinary folk in the past as research continues in the coming decades.

87 *Fieldwork at Shapwick: making out the labels and preparing the maps, (top left); fieldwalking a ploughed field looking for finds, (top right); washing finds at one of our cottages, (bottom left); a selection of Roman finds from one field, pottery on the left, coin in the centre and bone on the right, (bottom right)*

9 Favourite sites and museums

I have spent a great deal of my free time over the last thirty years travelling around different parts of Europe looking at well-known sites and visiting museums but also, when I had the information to hand, looking at the lesser known and therefore generally the more typical mundane monuments.

I used to camp a lot with a small canvas tent, but since 1978 I have had a succession of vans which I have used as campers – firstly two of the Volkswagen type IIs with the water-cooled engine. I bought my first van after seeing German families in Crete in March, in the rain, cooking meals and making coffee, while I was out in the weather getting bronchitis. As with every other owner I know I had the engine explode at 100,000 miles, in my case at Utrecht in Holland on the way back from visiting sites in Denmark.

Since 1990 I have had a four-wheel drive Volkswagen Transporter (Synchro) (**88**), a rare beast which is the ultimate fieldworking machine. It will easily do 70 mph, it can be driven up tracks and across ploughed fields, but I can also sleep and cook in it, and brew coffee wherever I want. It starred in my *Time Traveller* series for HTV as a sort of 'Tardis' taking me from site to site. It has enabled me to see many sites in only one day and I can travel at night and then camp without needing to find campsites or book into hotels. It is an ideal vehicle and I cannot imagine anything better – it does everything I want.

88 *The ultimate fieldwork machine. With my son James and the Volkswagen Transporter Synchro in Brittany in 1992.* Carinne Allinson

89 *Stonehenge in May 1986, more or
less as I saw it in 1963*

   With these vans I have spent over twenty years visiting sites in Britain and
all the neighbouring European countries, France, Belgium, the Netherlands,
Germany and Denmark. I have been to see sites of all periods in France, but
especially monasteries. Lately I have returned to Cornwall, Wales and
Scotland, rediscovering places I had been before but seeing them in a new
light after so much field experience elsewhere.
   My greatest discovery, over the last five years, has been Ireland, an amazing
country full of the most wonderful archaeology (people and pubs). Why
didn't I discover it before? Now I go back at least once a year, especially to the
wild empty west coast counties of Cork, Kerry, Clare and Galway (**32** & **33**).
   After all I have said so far in this book you may be surprised to know that I
am still impressed by the major sites of archaeology when I visit them. It is
impossible *not* to be impressed and overawed by the great world tourist
attractions. They are justly famous because they are so awe inspiring. But they
are not usually my *favourite* sites. As I have tried to show these are more likely
to be the everyday settlement sites where ordinary people lived and worked.
So there is a difference between what I am impressed and overawed by and
what I am interested in and would like to do research on.
   The first sites everyone should go and visit are those with a very high

90   The Great Pyramid of Cheops in Egypt on my visit in 1978

WOW! factor. Sites which are so old or large or magnificent that they are overwhelming to visit. Obvious ones that I have visited are Stonehenge (**89**), the Pyramids in Egypt (**90**), the Akropolis in Athens (**91**), and Knossos on Crete (**92**), though I am sure this list should also include Machu Picchu (Peru), Rome (Italy), Olduvai Gorge (Tanzania), Great Zimbabwe (Zimbabwe), Jerusalem (Israel), Angkor (Cambodia) and Constantinople (Turkey), which I haven't visited yet. I would also like to include the Minoan town at Akrotiri on the Greek island of Santorini (**93**). This, in my opinion, is better than Pompeii in Italy but I would include the site there together with (the rather better) Herculaneum (**94**). Both of these Roman cities were buried in volcanic debris when Mount Vesuvius blew up in AD 79. Equally impressive are the great Neolithic tombs (**95**) of Maes Howe (Orkney), Gavrinis (Brittany) and New Grange (Ireland), all huge and decorated. The other great Irish passage tomb at Knowth *should* be included but its megalithic art (the largest collection in Europe) is not accessible to the public.

Prehistoric sites are often less impressive but Lascaux would be amazing to visit (I have never been in the caves). The bodies preserved in the Danish bogs, especially Tollund Man (in Silkeborg Museum) and Grauballe Man (in Moesgard, Aarhus) (**96**) had a stunning effect on me; it's rare to look at someone from prehistory face to face.

91   The Parthenon, on the Acropolis, in Athens. I first went there in 1978

For size, significance and strong impression I would include the North Wales Edwardian castles of Harlech, Caernarvon and especially Conwy (**97**). These were the equivalent of the cruise missiles of today, the greatest expenditure and the latest in military technology. On the peaceful medieval front the remains of the abbeys at Cîteaux, Cluny and Clairvaux, and the monastery at La Grande Chartreuse are out of all proportion to the pan-European importance they had in the Middle Ages (**68**).

For the more recent periods, *Mary Rose* (**98**), Henry VIII's Tudor wooden battleship at Portsmouth, together with its contents is a staggering sight in its plastic (conservation) time capsule.

Mind-boggling museums, mainly because they are full of treasure which it is difficult not to be impressed by, include, of course, the British Museum (with for example the Sutton Hoo treasure), the Ashmolean Museum in Oxford (with the Alfred jewel), the National Museum in Athens and the Museum at Irakleion (on Crete), and the National Museum in Dublin with its vast collection of prehistoric gold, early Christian treasures and Viking finds from Dublin itself. The National Museum of Wales (at Cardiff) also has amazing finds but the peculiar building and display scheme in the National Museum of Scotland (in Edinburgh) make it difficult, I found, to appreciate the richness of the collections there. Generally I object to having to pay to see some of these collections of our communal heritage; they should be maintained from our general taxation.

92 *Knossos, Crete, Greece. Standing beside a pithos (storage pot) in the great magazines (storage warehouses) in the west range of the Minoan palace, March 1978*

93 The amazing excavated Bronze Age settlement at Akrotiri on Santorini, Greece. I am standing next to a three-storey building of around 1800 BC. October 1978

94 On the left a view over the part of the town of Herculaneum next to the beach and below are the mills and ovens of a bakery and shop in Pompeii. September 1987

95 *The big Neolithic burial chambers: Gavrinis, Brittany, the decorated stones of the passage to the burial chamber, (above left); New Grange, Ireland, the entrance to the passage, with the 'light box' above and blocking decorated slab in front, (above right); Maes Howe, Orkney, inside the burial chamber in the centre of the mound, (left)*

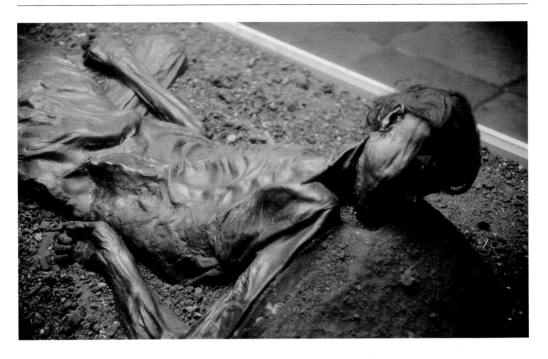

96 *Grauballe Man in the museum at Moesgard, Aarhus, Denmark. He was preserved in the acid conditions of a bog for 2000 years*

Beyond these sites and museums of European significance there are sites in almost every country and region which are of more than local significance and which never fail to impress. In Britain, in my region the complex at Avebury (in Wiltshire) of the Avebury circles and avenues, Silbury Hill and West Kennet long barrow, and the hillforts at South Cadbury and Maiden Castle. Elsewhere, Grimes Graves early prehistoric flint mines, the Roman spring, temple and baths at Bath, Hadrian's Wall with the forts at Housesteads, Birdoswald and Vindolanda, the latter with an amazing collection of ordinary Roman letters on wooden writing tablets, Danebury hillfort, Skara Brae neolithic village on Orkney, Tintern, Rievaulx, Fountains and Melrose Cistercian abbeys, the great houses at Blenheim and Castle Howard, the early gardens at Stourhead (Wiltshire) and Levens Hall (Lancashire), the Beam Engine in Birmingham City Museum (in steam) and the aeroplane collection at Duxford in Cambridgeshire.

I particularly like museums where there are replica or re-erected structures and where a three dimensional view of the past can be gained. Some of the best are in Europe (**99**), like Samara (near Amiens, Somme in northern France), the Archaeodrome (near Dijon France) and the Archaeosite in Belgium. In the British Isles the Craggaunowen Centre (**100**) in Clare,

97 *Edward I's great fortresses in the North Wales built in the late thirteenth century. On the left, Conwy, one of the great towers overlooking the walled town and harbour; on the right, the Eagle Tower at Caernarvon*

Ireland, is similar and here is kept Tim Severin's replica boat, the Brendan, built to follow St Brendan's voyage to North America in early Christian times. In Britain my favourites are Butser in Hampshire (**43**), Flag Fen near Peterborough, Cranborne in Dorset, the 'Celtic Village' near Greenbottom in Cornwall and Castell Henllys in Pembrokeshire (**44**).

Otherwise sites and landscapes where I feel I can get close to the ordinary people of the past are the places I like best. It will be clear from much of this book that it is not so much the rulers and their large burial and ceremonial monuments that interest and impress me personally but rather the evidence for the lives of *most* of the population in the past. Inevitably then I am likely to be more excited by ordinary sites and their contemporary landscapes.

98 *The* Mary Rose, *Henry VIII's great battleship being conserved (kept wet) in its plastic tent in Portsmouth dockyard*

Everywhere in this country, and in any country of course, there are examples which could be included here. In any average parish (if such actually exists because the great joy is the diversity and complexity of almost anywhere), there may be prehistoric barrows, early earthworks such as hillforts, rarely some exposed Roman remains, little of Anglo-Saxon date, a good medieval church, possible settlement earthworks, early houses from the late medieval, sixteenth- or seventeenth-century date, industrial remains of quarries, mines, engines, lime kilns and so on, bits of canal, early road alignments and holloways, abandoned railways, and collections of vernacular farmstead buildings.

Such sites and features are more typical of the lives of the vast majority of people in the past. They are everyday, local, ordinary, commonplace, typical

141

99 *Reconstructed and replica sites in Europe:*
The front of a replica Neolithic house at the Archaeosite in Belgium (top left);
and the view inside a similar replica house at the Samara site, near Amiens (Somme), France, with its
hearth, oven, pottery and working areas, (bottom right).
Replica Iron Age houses inside the great 'organic' concrete shell at Samara, (bottom left);
and the replica of Caesar's siege-works at Alesia, erected full size, with towers, palisades, ditches and pits
at the Archaeodrome near Dijon, Burgundy, France, (top right)

100 *The Craggaunowen Centre, County Clare, Ireland, which has many replica structures: a crannog settlement with its artificial island, bridge and houses (above); and Tim Severin's replica of an early medieval boat, the Brendan, in its perspex dome (right)*

and unexceptional. They do not represent wealth, power, significant historical events and have little to do with the richest levels of society. As such I find them the most interesting and exciting sites it is possible to visit. Give me a peasant house rather than a pyramid any day.

10 Favourite books and recommended reading

It is *not* my intention to give a full bibliography with footnotes and recommended texts but the reader may find it useful to follow up some of the chapters with a few selected books.

There are many good *general* books in archaeology. Perhaps the best available is Kevin Greene, *Archaeology: An Introduction* (Routledge 1995) though essential for reference is Colin Renfrew and Paul Bahn, *Archaeology: Theories, Methods and Practice* (Thames and Hudson 1991). (Anything by Paul Bahn is worth reading – see also his *Archaeology: A Very Short Introduction* (Oxford 1996), his excellent *Bluff your Way in Archaeology* (Ravette Books 1989) and, with Bill Tidy, *Disgraceful Archaeology or Things you shouldn't know about the history of mankind* (Tempus 1999).)

Modesty does not prevent me from mentioning *The Atlas of Archaeology –The Definitive Guide to the Location, History and Significance of the World's Most Important Archaeological Sites and Finds* (WOW!) by Mick Aston and Tim Taylor (Dorling Kindersley 1998). The most recent survey of British archaeology is *The Archaeology of Britain* edited by John Hunter and Ian Ralston (Routledge 1999).

1 Early years in archaeology

A flavour of the influence of Philip Rahtz can be gained from his *Introduction to Archaeology* (Blackwell 1985) and the essays by his friends and colleagues (including me on the Carthusians) in *In Search of Cult: Archaeological Investigations in Honour of Philip Rahtz* (edited by Martin Carver, The Boydell Press 1993).

2 Spreading the word

Much of the story of *Time Team* has been told by Tim Taylor in his fine *Behind the Scenes at Time Team* with superb photographs by Chris Bennett (Channel 4 Books 1998), and his follow up *The Ultimate Time Team Companion* (Channel

4 Books 1999). Julian Richards book *Meet the Ancestors: Unearthing the Evidence that Brings us Face to Face with the Past* (BBC 1999) also shows how television is depicting archaeology today.

3 Landscape archaeology

W G Hoskins, *The Making of the English Landscape* is still essential reading especially the 1988 edition with notes by Christopher Taylor. My own approach to fieldwork and the landscape is covered in *Landscape Archaeology* with Trevor Rowley (David and Charles 1974) and *Interpreting the Landscape* (Routledge 1985).

Fieldwork is also covered well in a number of books by Chris Taylor *Fieldwork in Medieval Archaeology* (Batsford 1974), *Fields in the English Landscape* (Dent 1975), *Roads and Tracks of Britain* (Dent 1979): see also Tony Brown, *Fieldwork for Archaeologists and Local Historians* (Batsford 1987) and Mark Bowden (ed), *Unravelling the Landscape* (Tempus / RCHM 1999).

There are a number of books on air survey but the best, I think, is still David Wilson *Air Photo Interpretation for Archaeologists* (Batsford 1982; 2nd ed. Tempus 2000). Most counties also now have a volume on sites from the air – one of the best is Frances Griffith's *Devon's Past: An Aerial View* (Devon Books 1988); see also Robert Croft and M Aston, *Somerset from the Air* (Somerset County Council 1993).

4 Archaeology and science

Much of the research on science in archaeology is reported in articles in journals and the text books tend to lag behind the discoveries. The following is a selection:

John Evans, *The Environment of Early Man in the British Isles* (Paul Elek 1975) is still very useful but also see his *Land and Archaeology* (Tempus 1999); Martin Jones, *England Before Domesday* (Batsford 1986) and *The Environment in British Prehistory* edited by Ian Simmons and Michael Tooley (Duckworth 1981) and IG Simmons, *Environmental History: A Concise Introduction* (Blackwell 1993) are good. For the Somerset Levels see Bryony and John Coles, *Sweet Track to Glastonbury: The Somerset Levels in Prehistory* (Thames and Hudson 1986) and their *People of the Wetlands: Bogs, Bodies and Lake Dwellers* (Guild Publishing 1989).

Anthony Clark, *Seeing Beneath the Soil: Prospecting Methods in Archaeology* (Batsford 1990) is the best general available account of geophysical methods. Mike Baillie's book on tree-ring dating, *A Slice Through Time: Dendrochronology and Precision Dating* (Batsford 1995) is now followed by his bombshell, *Exodus to Arthur: Catastrophic Encounters with Comets* (Batsford 1999).

For human remains see Don Brothwell, *The Bog Man and the Archaeology of People* (British Museum Publications 1986) and John Prag and Richard Neave, *Making Faces* (British Museum 1999). Dealing with skeletons and other human remains is covered in *Studies in Crime: An Introduction to Forensic Archaeology* by John Hunter, Charlotte Roberts and Anthony Martin (Batsford 1996). Just what can be achieved from modern scientific examination of archaeological remains can be seen in Konrad Spindler, *The Man in the Ice* (Weidenfeld and Nicholson 1994), *The Greenland Mummies*, edited by Jans Peder, Hant Hansen and others (British Museum 1991), *Lindow Man: The Body in the Bog*, I M Stead and others (Guild Publishing 1986) and *Bog Bodies: New Discoveries and New Perspectives* edited by R C Turner and R G Scaife (British Museum 1995).

5 Experimental archaeology

John Coles, *Archaeology by Experiment* (Hutchinson 1973) was the pioneering book; Peter Reynolds, *Iron Age Farm: The Butser Experiment* (British Museum Publications 1979) is still useful. Flag Fen is covered in Francis Pryor, *Flag Fen: Prehistoric Fenland Centre* (Batsford / English Heritage 1991) and his *Farmers in Prehistoric Britain* (Tempus 1998). The best book of all is however Jake Keen, *A Teacher's Guide to Ancient Technology* (English Heritage 1996).

There seems to be nothing in book form which covers re-enactment societies and their activities but see Ken and Denise Guest, *British Battles: the Front Lines of History in Colour Photographs* (Harper Collins / English Heritage 1996).

6 The archaeology of buildings

The book that helped to start Buildings Archaeology is Maurice Barley, *The English Farmhouse and Cottage* (Routledge and Kegan Paul 1961); there are now large numbers of local studies for counties: The Pevsner *Buildings of England* (and Wales, Scotland and Ireland) series are essential glove-box sources. Farm buildings are less well covered but R W Brunskill, *Traditional Farm Buildings of Britain* (Gollancz 1987) is useful. Warwick Rodwell, *Church Archaeology* (Batsford / English Heritage 1989) is the standard work on church archaeology.

7 Monasteries

The essential lists of monastic sites are contained in D Knowles and R N Hadcock, *Medieval Religious Houses: England and Wales* (Longman 1971), I B Cowan and D E Easson, *Medieval Religious Houses: Scotland* (Longman 1976) and A Gwynn and R N Hadcock, *Medieval Religious Houses: Ireland* (Irish Academic Press 1970).

Good recent general books include: Glyn Coppack, *Abbeys and Priories* (Batsford / English Heritage 1990), *The White Monks: The Cistercians in Britain 1128-1540* (Tempus 1998), J Patrick Greene, *Medieval Monasteries* (Leicester University Press 1992), Roberta Gilchrist, *Gender and Material Culture: The Archaeology of Religious Women* (Routledge 1994) and *Contemplation and Action: The Other Monasticism* (Leicester University Press 1995) and my own *Monasteries* (Batsford 1993, 2nd ed. Tempus 2000).

8 Medieval settlements in Somerset and the Shapwick Project

Deserted villages are covered in Maurice Beresford, *The Lost Villages of England* (Lutterworth 1954), *Deserted Medieval Villages*, edited by Maurice Beresford and John Hurst (Lutterworth 1971) and Richard Muir, *The Lost Villages of Britain* (Michael Joseph 1982): Wharram Percy in Maurice Beresford and John Hurst, *Wharram Percy, Deserted Medieval Village* (Batsford / English Heritage 1990).

Medieval settlements are covered in *The Rural Settlements of Medieval England*, edited by M Aston, David Austin, and Christopher Dyer (Blackwell 1989) but best of all in Christopher Taylor's fine *Village and Farmstead: A History of Rural Settlement in England* (George Philip 1983).

The work on Shapwick is not yet published fully. A summary can be found in *Current Archaeology* 151 (published February 1997) and on the web at: *www.wkac.ac.uk/shapwick*

Finally a few books which might not be the *easiest* to read and understand but which for me have provided great mental stimulation – these are the books which have often set me off with enthusiasm on new trains of thought.

John Harvey, *Medieval Gardens* (Batsford 1981). I haven't said much about early gardens which are another of my interests but this is the book which details the plants that were available and the styles of garden.

David Knowles, *The Monastic Order in England* (Cambridge 1963) – the book for sorting out what happened in monasticism in England.

J V Luce, *The End of Atlantis: New Light on an Old Legend*, (1970). An out-of-date book, but interesting for the light it throws on the beginnings of the Santorini research.

Colin Morris, *The Papal Monarchy: The Western Church from 1050 to 1250* (Clarendon Press Oxford 1989), on the background to the medieval church.

Richard Morris, *Churches in the Landscape* (Dent 1989). A lovely book about the origins and development of churches.

Oliver Rackham, *The History of the Countryside* (Dent 1986). The best book available about why much of the landscape looks like it does.

Colin Renfrew, *Approaches to Social Archaeology* (Edinburgh University Press 1984) – an ideas book which I have found very thought-provoking over the years.

Colin Renfrew and Malcolm Wagstaff (eds), *An Island Polity: The Archaeology of Exploitation in Melos* (Cambridge 1982). A good example of how modern archaeologists look at an area (an island, in this case, but it applies equally to a parish) and unravel how it has developed.

Marshall Sahlins, *Stone Age Economics* (Tavistock Publications 1984). A refreshing book showing that our modern economic system is only one of a very large number of ways of arranging exchange between people.

Joseph Tainter, *The Collapse of Complex Societies* (Cambridge 1982). A great summary of how societies have collapsed – perhaps a lot of lessons for us.

Acknowledgments

Many people have contributed to this book either directly or by their influence and example. I am particularly grateful to Philip Rahtz who initially got me into archaeology, to influential colleagues who encouraged a less than confident student and then field archaeologist – Robin Donkin, Philip Barker, Trevor Rowley, Graham Webster, Don Benson and Barry Cunliffe. Once launched I was greatly helped by Peter Fowler (at Bristol), Russell Lillford and Tony Haskell (at Taunton) Dick Smethurst and Geoffrey Thomas (in Oxford).

Once back in Bristol I have been grateful to my colleagues for assistance at the University, the late Geoffrey Cunliffe, Liz Bird, Joe Bettey and Michael Costen, and in Somerset, Ian Burrow and Bob Croft. At Shapwick, Paula Gardiner, Shirley Everden, Harry Jelley, Dennis Hill-Cottingham, Sue Fitton, Teresa Hall and many others who have born the brunt of the fieldwork (and bad weather).

I owe my television career to Tim Taylor but *Time Team* only works because of my other good friends on the programme, Tony Robinson, Phil Harding, Carenza Lewis, Victor Ambrus, Robin Bush and all the rest of the crews, archaeologists, technicians and production people involved. They are a great group to work with and have become my extended 'family' in a very real sense.

Any academic is only effective with good secretaries; over the years Valerie Camp, Carinne Allinson, Jane Geeson, Celia Bennetts, Deb Blackman, and now Helen Delingpole have been my University secretaries, and good former and current post-graduate research students – Chris Gerrard, Jenni Butterworth, Lee Prosser, and now Andrew Eden, Andrew Jackson, Sarah Whittingham, Nick Corcos and Magnus Alexander.

For permission to use photographs I am very grateful to Carinne Allinson, Chris Bennett, Bob Croft, John Dallimore, Graham Dixon, Teresa Hall and Peter Hardy. The rest came from my own vast slide collection. I owe a great debt to my old friend Martin Elliot (who took the famous picture of the 'Tennis Girl', the poster of which was on the wall of every male student) for the cover picture.

For keeping 'normal' life going and for providing the infrastructure so that I could have the time to write, travel and take part in *Time Team*, I owe a special debt to my mother, Glad Aston, my children, James Aston and Katherine Allinson, and also to John Hudson and Trudy Mansfield, Joe Cornish, Barry Wheeler, David John, Sue Fitton, Archie and Marie Forbes (for the sloe gin), and in the University, Mark Horton, Michael Costen and Mark Corney.

Finally to my PA Teresa Hall, for all her work and careful editing of this book and for her good advice when I was uncertain what the public might like.

This book would not have been possible without all these people. It is dedicated to them and to all my students – undergraduates, continuing education class members, *Time Team* supporters and television viewers.

Appendix I – Television programmes

Time Signs

Programme Title	Broadcast date
The Deserted Valley	30 June 1991
The Lost Village	7 July 1991
The Turning Wheel	14 July 1991
The Final Harvest	21 July 1991

Produced and directed by Tim Taylor. A Videotext Communications Production for Channel 4 Television.

Time Team

Pilot programme, Dorchester on Thames, Oxfordshire, made October 1992

Series 1	Programme recorded	Broadcast date
Much Wenlock, Shropshire	9-11 April 1993	30 January 1994
Athelney, Somerset	16-18 April 1993	16 January 1994
Ribchester, Lancashire	4-6 September 1993	23 January 1994
Llangorse, Powys	16-18 September 1993	6 February 1994

Series 2	Programme recorded	Broadcast date
Tockenham, Wiltshire	23-25 April 1994	22 January 1995
Winterbourne Gunner, Wilts	6-8 May 1994	15 January 1995
Hylton, Sunderland	10-12 June 1994	15 February 1995
Finlaggan, Islay	24-26 June 1994	8 January 1995
Lambeth Palace, London	8-10 July 1994	29 January 1995

Series 3

	Programme recorded	Broadcast date
Boleigh, Cornwall	17-19 March 1995	7 January 1996
Navan, County Armagh	7-9 April 1995	4 February 1996
Stanton Harcourt, Oxon	21-23 April 1995	14 January 1996
Templecombe, Somerset	26-28 May 1995	21 January 1996
Teignmouth, Devon	30 June-2 July 1995	28 January 1996
Preston St Mary, Suffolk	28-30 Aug 1995	11 February 1996

Series 4

	Programme recorded	Broadcast date
Launceston, Cornwall	22-24 March 1996	12 January 1997
Birmingham	5-7 April 1996	19 January 1997
Maryland, USA	17-19 May 1996	5 January 1997
Govan, Glasgow	14-16 June 1996	26 January 1997
Malton, North Yorkshire	5-7 July 1996	2 February 1997
Netheravon, Wiltshire	2-4 Aug 1996	9 February 1997

Series 5

	Programme recorded	Broadcast date
Greylake, Somerset	17-19 March 1997	11 January 1998
Mallorca, Spain	9-11 May 1997	1 February 1998
Orkney, Scotland	7-9 June 1997	18 January 1998
Aston Eyre, Shropshire	27-29 June 1997	8 February 1998
Richmond, Surrey	25-27 July 1997	4 January 1998
Turkdean, Gloucestershire	23-25 August 1997	25 January 1998
Turkdean Live	23-25 August 1997	23-25 August 1997
Downpatrick, Co. Down	19-21 September 1997	22 February 1998
High Worsall, North Yorks.	10-12 October 1997	1 March 1998
Christmas Special		28 December 1997

Series 6

	Programme recorded	Broadcast date
Papcastle, Cumbria	13-15 March 1998	10 January 1999
Thetford, Norfolk	24-26 March 1998	17 January 1999
Plympton, Devon	15-17 April 1998	31 January 1999
Cheddar, Somerset	23-25 April 1998	24 January 1999

Smallhythe, Kent	2-4 June 1998	7 February 1999
Burslem, Stoke on Trent	8-10 June 1998	3 January 1999
Beauport Park, Sussex	19-21 June 1998	14 February 1999
Reedham, Norfolk	29 June-1 July	21 February 1999
Bawsey, Norfolk	29-31 August 1998	14 March 1999
Bawsey Live	29-31 August 1998	29-31 August 1998
Kemerton, Worcestershire	29 Sept-1 Oct 1998	2 March 1999
Turkdean, Gloucestershire	6-8 October 1998	28 February 1999
Nevis, West Indies	22-30 October 1998	21 March 1999
Nevis, West Indies	22-30 October 1998	28 March 1999

Series 7	Programme recorded	Broadcast date
Basing, Hampshire	30 March -1 April 1999	20 February 2000
Coventry, West Midlands	15-17 April 1999	13 February 2000
Waddon, Dorset	27-29 April 1999	23 January 2000
Flag Fen, Cambridgeshire	18-20 May 1999	27 February 2000
Wierre-Effroy, France	1-3 June 1999	16 January 2000
Cirencester, Gloucestershire	10-12 June 1999	9 January 2000
Birdoswald, Cumbria	27-29 June 1999	30 January 2000
Elveden, Suffolk	5-7 July 1999	6 February 2000
Greenwich, London	13-15 July 1999	12 March 2000
York	3-5 September 1999	26 March 2000
York Live	3-5 September 1999	3-5 September 1999
Hartlepool, Durham	20-22 September 1999	19 March 2000
Denia, Spain	30 Sept - 2 Oct 1999	2 January 2000
Sutton, Hereford	11 - 13 October 1999	5 March 2000
Christmas Special	3 December 1999	19 December 1999

'Seahenge', Norfolk – *Time Team* documentary to be shown on 29 December 1999

History Hunters

Programme	Broadcast at 4pm on
Crystal Palace	21 November 1998
Blackpool	28 November 1998

Nottingham	5 December 1998
Coventry	12 December 1998
Border Rievers★	19 December 1998
Burton Abbey★	2 January 1999
Marshfield★	9 January 1999

★ The programmes in which I took part.
Series producer, Tim Taylor. Series director, Jeremy Cross.
A Videotext Communications Production in association with The Picture House TV Co. for Channel 4 Television.

Time Traveller

First Series – half hour each. Made Sept 1996 - June 1997

	Director	Broadcast Date
In Search of Cheddar Man	Philip Priestley	7 July 1997
The Severn Estuary	Philip Priestley	21 July 1997
Low Ham	Harvey Lilley	28 July 1997
Deserted Medieval Villages	Harvey Lilley	4 August 1997
Avebury - Sacred Landscape	Harvey Lilley	11 August 1997
New Towns of the Middle Ages	Philip Priestley	18 August 1997

An Epik production for HTV.

Appendix 2 – Experimental archaeology and reconstructions

The following are sites with reconstructed replica early buildings and structures and those where experimental archaeology takes place.

Ancient Technology Centre, Cranborne Middle School, Cranborne, Dorset, BH21 5RP

Arbeia Roman Fort, Baring Street, South Shields, NE33 2BB

Bede's World, Jarrow Hall, Church Bank, Jarrow, NE32 3DY

Butser Ancient Farm, Nexus House, Gravel Hill, Horndean, Hampshire, PO8 0QE

Castell Henllys, Felindre Farchog, Newport, Pembrokeshire, SA41 3UT

Cornwall Celtic Village, Saveock Mill, Greenbottom, Truro, TR4 8QQ

Cosmeston Medieval Village, Cosmeston Country Park, Laverlock Road, Penarth, Vale of Glamorgan, CF64 5UY

Lunt Roman Fort, Coventry Road, Baginton, Coventry

Peat Moors Visitor Centre, Shapwick Road, Westhay, Glastonbury, Somerset, BA6 9TT

West Stow Country Park, Bury St Edmunds, IP28 6HE

Welsh Folk Museum, St Fagans, Cardiff, CF5 6XB

Index

The page numbers of illustrations are indicated in **bold** type.